Selected Poems
JOHN CIARDI

Selected
Poems

JOHN CIARDI

The University of Arkansas Press
Fayetteville

Hum
PS
3505
I27
A6
1984

Designer: Patricia Douglas Crowder
Typeface: Linotron 202 Sabon
Typesetter: G & S Typesetters, Inc.
Printer: Thomson-Shore, Inc.
Binder: John H. Dekker & Sons, Inc.

The author wishes to express his grateful acknowledgment to
W. W. Norton Co. for permission to include poems from *For Instance*
by John Ciardi; © 1978.
LIBRARY OF CONGRESS CATALOGING-IN-PUBLICATION DATA

CIARDI, JOHN, 1916–
SELECTED POEMS.

I. TITLE.
PS3505.I27A6   1984   811'.52   83-24254
ISBN 0-938626-29-9
ISBN 0-938626-30-2 (PBK.)

for John Holmes
and Roy W. Cowden
in loving gratitude.

Also by John Ciardi

Homeward to America
Other Skies
Live Another Day
From Time to Time
Mid-Century American Poets (Anthology)
As If
Poems New and Selected
I Marry You
39 Poems
How Does a Poem Mean? (with Williams)
In the Stoneworks
In Fact
This Strangest Everything
Lives of X
Dialogue with an Audience
Poetry, a Closer Look (with Reid and Perrine)
Person to Person
An Alphabestiary
The Little That Is All
Manner of Speaking
Limericks, Too Gross
A Grossery of Limericks
For Instance
A Browser's Dictionary I
A Browser's Dictionary II

Books for children

The Reason for the Pelican
Scrappy the Pup
I Met a Man
The Man Who Sang the Sillies
You Read to Me, I'll Read to You
Someone Could Win a Polar Bear
The Wish-Tree
J. J. Plenty and Fiddler Dan
You Know Who
Fast and Slow
The Monster Den
The King Who Saved Himself from Being Saved

Translation

Dante's Divine Comedy

Contents

LIVES OF X

TRIBAL POEMS

The Evil Eye

(The belief in the Evil Eye is a still-surviving superstition
among Italian peasants. One method of detecting its presence
is to pour olive oil on a saucer of holy water. The shapes
assumed by the oil can then be read by the gifted.)

Nona poured oil on the water and saw the eye
    Form on my birth. Zia beat me with bay
    Fennel and barley to scourge the devil away.
I doubt I needed so much excuse to cry.

From Sister Maria Immaculata there came
    A crucifix, a vow of nine days' prayer,
    And a scapular stitched with virgin's hair.
The eye glowed on the water all the same.

By Felice, the midwife, I was hung with a tin
    Fish stuffed with garlic and bread crumbs.
    Three holy waters washed the breast for my gums.
Still the eye glared, wide as original sin

On the deepest pools of women midnight-spoken
    To ward my clamoring soul from the clutch of hell,
    Lest growing I be no comfort and dying swell
More than a grave with horror. Still unbroken

The eye glared through the roosts of all their clucking.
    "Jesu," cried Mother, "why is he deviled thus?"
    "Baptism without delay," said Father Magnus.
"This one is not for sprinkling but for ducking."

So in came meat and wine and the feast was on.
    I wore a palm frond in my lace, and sewn
    To my swaddling band a hoop and three beads of bone
For the Trinity. And they ducked me and called me John.

And ate the meat and drank the wine, and the eye
    Closed on the water. All this fell between
    My first scream and first name in 1916,
The year of the war and the influenza, when I

Was not yet ready for evil or my own name,
Though I had one already and the other came.

Bridal Photo, 1906

A ceremonial rose in the lapel,
a horseshoe wreath of pearls in the tie-knot,
a stone-starched collar bolted at the throat,
a tooth on a gold chain across the vest—
this is the man, costumed for solemn taking.

Pompadoured and laced and veiled for giving,
the woman sits her flower-time at his side
badged with his gifts—gold watch on a fleur-de-lis
pin at the heart, gold locket at the throat—
her hand at total rest under his hand.

What moment is this frozen from their lives
as if a movie stuck in its lit tracks?
Between the priest's gilt cave and their new bed,
ducking and giggling through the rowdy friends
who scattered rice and waited to get drunk,

they ran out of their day to the rigged cave
of the unknown hooded man who took their look
and made it into paper. Here they are:
stopped with all eyes upon them in his eye,
so solemn and so starched, they must have laughed

a thousand times, when they could laugh again,
to see themselves carved from themselves like stone.
And yet what moment is this of their lives
who hold their lives so open to all looking?
Was this the bridal and all else the dance?

Half-man, half-woman, not yet one another,
but in a first time and a last between
that separate morning and all joined good nights,
they stood to think their lives into one look
and hold the unfinished bridal to its hour.

Oh man and woman tranced in your new flowers,
your eyes are deep as churches, but as far
as you look out unseeing, the years look in!
Sweet strangers, I am left across your lives
to see the flower day taken from its flowers.

I follow this long look into its dark
where, leathered as an Indian chief, the woman
sags through this lace to keen for the bashed corpse
that drops from the man's steadiness in his hour.
I hold this study by the hooded man

and pray to that held hour from its last love:
  Bless the unfinished bridal to its bed.
  This day becomes this day. What others follow
  have touched their flower. By all flowers and all fall
  I am the son of this man and this woman.

Elegy

My father was born with a spade in his hand and traded it
for a needle's eye to sit his days cross-legged on tables
till he could sit no more, then sold insurance, reading
the ten-cent-a-week lives like logarithms from
the Tables of Metropolitan to their prepaid tombstones.

Years of the little dimes twinkling on kitchen tables
at Mrs. Fauci's at Mrs. Locatelli's at Mrs. Cataldo's
(*Arrividerla, signora. A la settimana prossima. Mi saluta,*
la prego, il marito. Ciao, Anna. Bye-bye.)
—known as a Debit. And with his ten-year button

he opened a long dream like a piggy bank, spilling the dimes
like mountain water into the moss of himself, and bought
ten piney lots in Wilmington. Sunday by Sunday
he took the train to his woods and walked under the trees
to leave his print on his own land, a patron of seasons.

I have done nothing as perfect as my father's Sundays
on his useless lots. Gardens he dreamed from briar tangle
and the swampy back slope of his ridge rose over him
more flowering than Brazil. Maples transformed to figs,
and briar to blood-blue grapes in his look around

when he sat on a stone with his wine-jug and cheese beside
    him,
his collar and coat on a branch, his shirt open,

his derby back on his head like a standing turtle. A big
man he was. When he sang *Celeste Aida* the woods
filled as if a breeze were swelling through them.

When he stopped, I thought I could hear the sound still
    moving.
—Well, I have lied. Not so much lied as dreamed it.
I was three when he died. It was someone else—my sister—
went with him under the trees. But if it was her
memory then, it became mine so long since

I will owe nothing on it, having dreamed it from àll
the nights I was growing, the wet-pants man of the family.
I have done nothing as perfect as I have dreamed him
from old-wives tales and the running of my blood.
God knows what queer long darks I had no eyes for

followed his stairwell weeks to his Sunday breezeways.
But I will swear the world is not well made that rips
such gardens from the week. Or I should have walked
a saint's way to the cross and nail by nail
hymned out my blood to glory, for one good reason.

It Took Four Flowerboats to Convoy My Father's Black

It took four flowerboats to convoy my father's black
Cadillac cruiser out to St. Mike's and down
deeper than all salt. It was a very successful
funeral my mother remembers remembering. *Imagine*
what flowers! Even the undertaker was surprised,
he told me! He came with only two flowercars.
He had to send his son all over town like crazy
to find two more, there were so many. Imagine!

And when the funeral went to circle the block three
times—those days they did that: it was like the man
coming home again three times for his soul to remember—
we started, and when the first cars came around, the last
were still blocking the street! Even
the undertaker was surprised! He had to go around two

6

blocks instead of one to make the circles for the soul!
You were too small to remember, but imagine!

. . . It was my first cruise: the streets ahead a groundswell
of flowers, the wind ripping petals like spume from a wave,
the hearse bobbing nattily in the troughs, powerful
and in ballast, dead into the flower-stripping wind, and steady.
Man! what a big day at sea it was in that wind past all
the shores that stood-to and moved with us through
the ports of the black cabin my mother made of her flesh
in the black Cadillac cruiser I midshipped in. I mean, God,

it was a regatta, I tell you, she told me,
half of which I remember, and half of which
I remember being told after I had forgotten it once.
There were thirty-three powerboats from the Figli d'Italia
alone; seventeen (sometimes nineteen, and once, twenty-seven)
from Metropolitan; and half the North End in the rest. That's
ninety, or over a hundred, and, some days, more, not
counting the flowerboats and the hearse.
                                    I had to go
(well, so I did, but I mean years later) to Venice and lean over
a cortege of gondolas stroked under the Ponte di Rialto
and out the big circle to the Campo Santo, like a trooping
of black swans on a fire-glaze, before I remembered clean
what an armada my father died into, sailing his flower-storm
        out
on the wind of the longest going my mother ever
sailed to sea or success on; and still breathes the forty-year-
old salt of new, between black and triumph.

Aunt Mary

Aunt Mary died of eating twelve red peppers
        after a hard day's work. The doctor said
        it was her high blood pressure finished her.
        As if disease were anything to Aunt Mary
        who had all of her habits to die of! But imagine
        a last supper of twelve red peppers, twelve

of those crab apple size dry scorchers
you buy on a string at Italian groceries,
twelve of them fried in oil and gobbled off
(Aunt Mary was a messy eater)—and then,
to feel the room go dizzy, and through your blood
the awful coming on of nothing more
than twelve red peppers you know you shouldn't have
    eaten
but couldn't help yourself, they were so good.

Now what shall I pray for gluttonous Aunt Mary
    who loved us till we screamed? Even poor Mother
had more of Aunt Mary's love than she could live with,
but had to live with it. I am talking now
of a house with people in it, every room
a life of a sort, a clutter of its own.
I am talking of a scene in the palm of God
in which one actor dies of twelve red peppers,
one has too many children, one a boy friend,
two are out of work, and one is yowling
for one (offstage) to open the bathroom door.
This is not the scene from the palm of God
in which the actors hold God in their palms,
nor the scene in which the actors know their prayers—

it is the scene in which Aunt Mary died
    and nobody knew anything, least of all
Aunt Mary. In her red-hot transformation
from gluttony into embalmer's calm
and candlelight, I cried a hypocrite tear.
But it was there, when I had seen Aunt Mary
bloodlet for God, that I began to see
what scene we are. At once I wept Aunt Mary
with a real tear, forgiving all her love,
and its stupidities, in the palm of God.
Or on a ledge of time. Or in the eye
of the blasting sun. Or tightroped on a theorem.
—Let every man select his own persuasion:
I pray the tear she taught me of us all.

Bedlam Revisited

Nobody told me anything much. I was born
free to my own confusions, though in hock
to Mother and Father Sweatshop's original stock
in Boston, Mass., four families to a john.
The spire of the Old North Church, like a tin horn
upside down on the roofs, was our kitchen clock,
and dropped the hours like rock onto a rock
over the Hull Street graveyard. "Gone. All gone,"

it thunked above the dead. The smells were sad.
And there were rats, of course, but nailed tin
could keep them down (or at least in)
to a noise between the hours. The graveyard had
left us a son in real estate and the lad
had grown to father our landlord, though Frank Glynn
was the wart-on-the-nose that came with a sneaky grin
to collect the rent. Till he died to Hell. Too bad.

Nobody told me anything much, and that
so wrong it cost me nothing—not even love—
to lose it. All but the Boss, the Cop and the Ghost of
the Irish Trinity. Those I sweated at
so hard I came up hating. But still grew fat
in a happy reek of garlic, bay, and clove.
I was crazy, of course, but always at one remove.
I tried on faces as if I were buying a hat.

Home was our Asylum. My father died
but my mother kept talking to him. My sisters screamed.
My aunt muttered. My uncle got drunk and dreamed
three numbers a night for a nickel with cock-eyed
Charlie Pipe-Dreams who moseyed along half-fried
every morning at seven. The old boy schemed
for twenty years that I knew of before he was reamed
by Family Morticians. But I'll say this—he tried.

Nobody told me anything much. Nobody had
anything much to tell me. I rolled my own
and scrounged for matches. How could I have known
everything about us was full-moon mad?
Or that I'd find few saner? It wasn't bad.

Someone always answered the telephone
when it had rung too long. You got only a tone
when they finally called you—far away and sad.
But it didn't matter. There would have been nothing to say.
Later they changed the number and we moved away.

Daemons

I pass enough savages on the street
to credit the daemon in things. But they
have forgotten how the soul breathes
from plant, beast, and man and must
be propitiated. They do avoid thirteenths,
walk wide of ladders and black cats,
make the sign of the cross for hearses.
But shabbily. Ritualists without conviction.

My mother, at bone and breath, was the savage
I learned from. When we poured
concrete for a new house, she leaned over
the half-filled forms muttering,
and dropped in a penny, a crucifix, a key,
then pricked her finger and shook out
a drop of blood. Then stood there,
waiting. Giving, had she given enough?

Because she meant to take no chances,
I thumbed a bean pod open and gave her
the beans, saying nothing, and she threw those
in. That started her going again. Off
she went to her kitchen and brought back
oil, wine, a sliver of meat, snippets
of all the food we had. In they went. Then
she thought a minute and told me to spit.

She was using everything she knew anything
about, and she knew she was using it. That
is my kind of savage. She was living at
the ghost of all she lived by.
Now suppose I say again I do

credit daemons? Suppose I pick up
a conch and blow it and ask if it hears
itself making music?—the idea loses you.

But there go the savages in and out of
Tiffany's, the Waldorf, the Cathedral,
the Subway. They take place; they do not
know themselves. They do, I suppose, move
to the music they think they hear. But
what I mean is—you have to hear your self
making the music you didn't know was
in you, living at what you live by.

The Lamb

A month before Easter
Came the time of the lamb
Staked on my lawn
To frisk and feed and be
My loveliest playmate,
Sweeter for being
Sudden and perilous.

Fed from my hand,
Brushed by my love,
A most acrid and gentle wool
Grew clumsy and beautiful.
The lamb is a beast of knees.
A dear and slender bleat
Quavers in it.

The eyes of the lamb
Are two damp surrenders
To the tears of the world:
The child must love
The lamb's total disarmament:
It is the first life to which man
Grew wholly superior.

Year by year the lamb
Danced the black Lenten season.
On the Thursday of sorrow
It disappeared.
On the Friday of blood I knew
What business was in the cellar
And wept a little.

But ah come Easter,
My lamb, my sufferer, rose,
From the charnel cellar,
Glowed golden brown
On religious plenty.
How gravely it was broken
Sprigged for a bridal.

I praise the soil
In the knuckle and habit
Of my feeding parents
Who knew anciently
How the holy and edible
Are one, are life, must be loved
And surrendered.

My tears for the lamb
Were the bath it sprang from
Washed and risen
To its own demand
For a defenseless death.
After the lamb had been wept for
Its flesh was Easter.

After Sunday Dinner We Uncles Snooze

Banana-stuffed, the ape behind the brain
scratches his crotch in nature and lies back,
one arm across his eyes, one on his belly.
Thanksgiving afternoon in Africa,
the jungle couches heaped with hairy uncles
between a belch and a snore. All's well that yawns.

12

Seas in the belly lap a high tide home.
A kind of breathing flip-flop, all arrival,
souses the world full in the sog of time,
lifting slopped apes and uncles from their couches
for the long drift of self to self. Goodbye:
I'm off to idiot heaven in a drowse.

This is a man. This blubbermouth at air
sucking its flaps of breath, grimacing, blowing,
rasping, whistling. Walked through by a zoo
of his own reveries, he changes to it.
His palm's huge dabble over his broken face
rubs out the carnivores. His pixie pout

diddles a butterfly across his lip.
His yeasty smile drools Edens at a spring
where girls from Bali, kneeling to their bath,
cup palms of golden water to their breasts.
His lower lip thrusts back the angry chiefs:
he snarls and clicks his teeth: "Stand back, by God!"

And so, by God, they do, while he descends
to rape those knobs of glory with a sigh,
then clouds, surceased, and drifts away or melts
into another weather of himself
where only a drowned mumble far away
sounds in his throat the frog-pond under time.

O apes and hairy uncles of us all,
I hear the gibberish of a mother tongue
inside this throat. (A prattle from the sea.
A hum in the locked egg. A blather of bloods.)
O angels and attendants past the world,
what shall the sleeps of heaven dream but time?

Three Views of a Mother

I

Good soul, my mother holds my daughter,
the onionskin bleached hand under the peach-head.
Ti-ti, she says from the vegetable world, *la-la*.
A language of roots from a forgotten garden.

She forms like a cresting wave over the child;
it is impossible not to see her break
and bury and the child swim up a girl
and the girl reach shore a woman on my last beach.

Ti-ti, la-la. I will not fight our drowning,
nor the fall of gardens. I am curious, however,
to know what world this is. The honeydew head
of the child, the cauliflower head of the grandmother

bob in the sea under the garden. *Ti-ti, la-la*.
The grandmother rustles her hands like two dry leaves
and the child writhes round as a slug for pleasure,
leaving the trail of its going wet on the world.

II

I see her in the garden, loam-knuckled in Spring,
urging the onions and roses up. Her hands
talk to the shoots in whispers, or in anger
they rip a weed away between thumb and fist.

When the jonquils open she makes a life of them.
Before the radishes come she is off to the fields,
scarved and bent like a gleaner, for dandelions.
When the beans are ready she heaps them in a bowl.

The Fall is lit by peaches. As if they were bubbles
she balances them from the branch and holds them out
one by one in her palm. Her eyes believe
the world self-evident in its creation.

Last of all the chrysanthemums take tongue
from the spikes of November. She lingers by glass boxes

14

coaxing the thickened earth a little longer
to hoard the sun for sprigs of mint and parsley.

But Winter comes and she is out of employment
and patience. She is not easy to be with
here by the buried garden. Winter mornings
she wakes like shrouded wax, already weary

of the iron day. *Ti-ti*, she says to the child,
la-la. A piece of her life. But her mind divides:
she knows there is seed enough for every forest,
but can she be sure there is time for one more garden?

III

Three rainy days and the fourth one sunny:
she was gone before breakfast. At three she hobbles back
under a flour sack bulging full of mushrooms.
Well, scolding will do no good. I see her eyes
hunting for praise as she fishes up a handful
and holds them to the light, then rips one open
for me to smell the earth in the white stem.

I think perhaps this woman is my child.
But right now what do we do with thirty pounds
of uncleaned mushrooms? If I let her be
she'll stay up cleaning them till one o'clock
and be all aches tomorrow. I get a knife;
and here we sit with the kitchen table between us,
one pile for root ends, one for the cleaned sprouts.

Her hands go back with her. I see her mind
open through fields from the earth of her stained fingers.
"Once when I was a girl I found a fungus
that weighed twenty-eight kilos. It was delicious.
I was going to Benevento for the fair.
I cut across the mountain to save time,
and there it was—like an angel in a tree.

"You don't see things like that. Not over here.
My father ran from the barn when I came home.
'Didn't you go to fair?' he said. But I laughed:
'I brought it home with me.' He wouldn't believe
I'd carried it all the way across the mountain,

and the path so steep. I made a sack of my skirt.
He thought some fellow—I don't know what he thought!"

Ti-ti. La-la. The memory works her fingers.
"Oh, we were happy then. You could go in the winter
and dig the roses and cabbages from the snow.
The land had a blessing. In the fall in the vineyards
we sang from dawn to sunset, and at night
we washed our feet and danced like goats in the grape vats.
The wine came up like blood between our toes."

We finish at last, the squid-gray fruit before us.
"Leave the root clippings," she says. "They're for the garden.
See how black the dirt is. Black's for growing."
She sets her hoard to soak. "I'm tired now.
Sometimes I talk too much. That's happiness.
Well, so we'll eat again before we die.
But oh, if you could have seen it in that tree!"

Epithalamium at St. Michael's Cemetery

My father lay fifty years in St. Michael's bed
till we laid back the covers and bundled in
the hag end of his lost bride, her wits shed
some years before her light. O, bones, begin
with one gold-banded bone. The bride is dressed
in tissue, ten claws folded on no breast.

Man and woman made he them, but gave
dominion to Dominion. Does He know
how deep the whale goes to its grave,
its hull of ribs still trembling in the flow
under the dark he makes there, or that is
unmade? If every deep is His,

then all bounds are abysses, as they were
when the set eyes of Sphinxes still stared through
their gilded doors to a green delta's stir
of rayed and hovering dynasts, while the Jew,
back at his interrupted captivity
in the ashes of lamentation, sang "Eli! Eli!"

16

What loss is this when nothing's left to lose?
She waited and she came, and he is there,
whether or not he waited. Can we choose
what we shall wait for? Can I find a tear
for what this is? I have none left. I see
a twice unfinished bridal. The chivaree

has been rescheduled. The Capuchin suite—
a grotto off the Via Veneto—
has been reserved for this first night, complete
with its two skeletal cupids flying low.
A crypt of the dead sea. There, side by side,
the sodden groom, the driftwood bride,

begin again forever what they began
in God's will, or the sand-blast through no door,
or the wind in the Jew's ashes, or as this man
and woman crossed their sea once, through whose floor
Capuchin birds silt into the abyss
He sets His bounds by. Or that simply is.

Alec

At ninety-seven my uncle found God heavy.
"My legs," he sighed, "May I go before they do."
So small an ambition: could it be asking too much
even from a universe? It or luck

spun him the answer he wanted. Sometimes we win.
I was in Asia and missed the funeral,
all but a postcard c/o AM. EX., BANGKOK.
I bought gold leaf and rubbed a Buddha for him,

my shoes at the door, with feet left to put in them.
His name was di Simone, which is "of Simon."
He could not read, but his family legend whispered
of a turned Jew centuries back. He married

my mother's sister and passed as Alec the Barber,
though really Alessio. The gold leaf crumbles.

It makes sparks on the floor like lathe-curlings.
But some of it sticks. In time the God turns gold

and we are all one family. Back in my shoes,
I fed beggars in his name for the plains-wide days
he walked me for quail or pheasant or what comes
in or out of season. "God," he would say

"sends birds, not calendars." He was right a while,
but calendars come, too. I must have loved him,
and did not know it till I fed beggars for him
and gilded an unfinished god in its vault.

S.P.Q.R. A Letter from Rome
Sono Porci Questi Romani

I

It does for the time of man to walk here
    by the spoken stones forgotten, a crisscrossed empire
    sticking its stumps out of cypress. Not a name,
    though stone-carved, but what a name
    is plastered over it. Not a god in town
    but watched his temple changed into a quarry.

And could smile: "Let them change Heaven and Earth
    if they can: nothing changes the Romans.
    Men as they were, beasts as they were, they are.
    Their God across the Tiber has stone arms
    stretched from his dome like crab's claws. Can claws hold
        them?
    Hundreds of kings have held Rome; none, the Romans.

Who knows the goats better than the goatherd?
    We piped their lambing from burnt rock
    and made a people of them. Rank and graceless
    they are a people yet. And ours. All arches
    are one to them. Whatever name is on them,
    they read their own. Exactly as we gave it."

—You hear that gods' pique everywhere. A jobless
    immortality fallen to sneers and gossip.

18

They'll rob you blind, kick your shins bloody,
elbow you over the edge, then smile and say "*Scusi.*"
History? Rome's no history, but a madhouse.
So, I suppose, the original of history.

It does for all of time to walk there
    over the unchanged changes—like a guard mount,
    the same before and after. What's there to change?
    You go to the Vatican or the Pantheon
    in the same mob.
                        And keep your pockets buttoned:
    leave one flap open—you'll learn history.

II

On stone, her stoned knees throbbing like a pulse
    in the concussion of holiness, Sister Pia,
    vowed to meditation, unwashed, unflinching,
    prayed in her stones that days and men be laundered.

"If I am worthy, teach me what I must suffer."
    Ten years upon her knees in the odor of grace.
    Spoon-fed a broth a day by those who cleaned her;
    the prayer bubbling on through every spoonful.

Ten years on her knees while the stone cell
    became a Colosseum and the blood
    steamed, hymned, to Heaven from the beasts'
    muzzles and the glory was said and said.

"If I am worthy, bless them." And was tolled
    by bells and the praying shadows of stone,
    the Convent black with triumph. —While, at the gates,
    a hundred thousand Fiats snarled and screeched.

III

Till one claxon of all rang statues quick:
    Mussolini ha sempre ragione. And he came
    out of the stones like yesterday-made-easy.
    A new statue sprung from every footfall.

Empire! And the mob remembered! It rained stone chips
    in Rome all one generation as the masons swung

again. A thousand, ten thousand, a million
  stone-thrust-chins for piazzas, dressers, export:

in the mud at Addis Ababa, an Arch of Triumph;
  in Libya, on the sand grill, a Colossus;
  across the Mare Nostrum in the moon,
  a bust of glory on the binnacle.

Till all hung upside down on a northern wall,
  suffered as Sister Pia to its stones, and the mob
  sang: "*Fatto! Viva l'America!*" Turned, praying:
  "If I am worthy—Joe, a cigarette."

IV

It does for the time of all to walk here
  by the saved arches and the forgotten surrenders.
  An empire of ego figging its thumbs at heaven.
  A museum of famines lurking to snatch bread.
  A propriety of dressed scorns promenading.
  A cradle of prayer bubbling.

As time is. Half a nonsense. Like a guard mount:
  the same stone godwatch before and after,
  a grandiose serenity with its lips cracked,
  smirking: "Let them change Heaven and Earth
  if they can. Nothing changes a Roman."

And still a marble marriage pomps the light.

An Apartment with a View

I am in Rome, Vatican bells tolling
a windowful of God and Bernini.
My neighbor, the Pope, has died
and God overnight, has wept
black mantles over the sainted
stone age whose skirted shadows
flit through to the main cave.

I nurse a cold. It must be error
to sniffle in sight of holiness.
"Liquids," the doctor said. He has
no cure, but since I have my choice,
I sip champagne. If I must sit
dropsical to Heaven, let me at least
be ritual to a living water.

In the crypt under the cave
the stone box in its stone row
has been marked for months now.
My neighbor knew where he was going.
I half suspect I, too, know,
and that it is nothing to sneeze at,
but am left to sneeze.

I drink my ritual Moët et Chandon
and wish (my taste being misformed
for the high authentic) I had
a California—a Korbel
or an Almaden. I like it "forward,"
as clerics of such matters say,
not schooled to greatness.

It is loud in Heaven today
and in the great stone school
my neighbor kept.
The alumni procession of saints
is forming for him. Bells
clobber the air with portents.
I sniffle and sneeze,

wad kleenex, and sip champagne,
trying to imagine what it might be
to take part in a greatness,
or even in the illusion
of something-like. The experience
might deepen my character,
though I am already near

the bottom of it, among wads and butts
of what was once idea. And the last swallow.
I do not like the aftertaste, if that

is what I am tasting. But this is ritual.
I toast my neighbor: may he
find his glass, and may its after-taste
be all that he was schooled to.

Poems from Italy

I

Nona Domenica Garnaro sits in the sun
    on the step of her house in Calabria.
    There are seven men and four women in the village
    who call her *Mama*, and the orange trees
    fountain their blooms down all the hill and valley.
    No one can see more memory from this step

than Nona Domenica. When she folds her hands
    in her lap they fall together
    like two Christs fallen from a driftwood shrine.
    All their weathers are twisted into them.
    There is that art in them that will not be carved
    but can only be waited for. These hands are not

sad nor happy nor tired nor strong. They are simply
    complete. They lie still in her lap
    and she sits waiting quietly in the sun
    for what will happen, as for example, a petal
    may blow down on the wind and lie across
    both of her thumbs, and she look down at it.

II

One day I went to look at the Mediterranean
and I found myself on an infected hill.
The waves under the sky and the sky over the waves
perfected themselves in endless repetition,
but the hill stumbled and twitched. A desert ate
into its sea front and a gully cankered
its piney back, or what had been
its piney back before that eczema

of stumps and stones and landslides. At its top
like a trollop's hat knocked cockeyed in a brawl
there leaned a tattered strawwork of gray grasses
that fizzed and popped with a plague of grasshoppers.
The grass was salt-burned and seemed wiry enough
to cut the hand that pulled it. And at its roots,
under the leaping gas of the live grasshoppers,
I saw a paste of the dead. There were so many
I thought at first it was the clay-sand soil
from which the wiregrass grew. I could not see
any of the living fall from their leaping
but the dead lay under them, a plague they made
invisibly of themselves who had come to feed
where the grass ate them on an infected hill.

And I saw there was no practice in the sea.

III

A man-face gathered on the eyes of a child
        measures me from an alleyway. The child
        stirs, but the face has lost its motion:
        the face stares at the traffic and the child
        picks with one finger at a scab on his knee.
        Not looking at it. Not knowing it is there.

He stares at me. I am part of what he knows.
        I am the traffic forever in his eyes
        and damnation, the way all worlds go
        leaving him neither admission nor understanding,
        as, somewhere in a thicket like the mind,
        a gargoyle might stare down at running water.

IV

You would never believe to watch this man
        open his pocket knife to cut his cheese
        (his bread he tears with his hands)
        and lay it down precisely on a leaf
        and tip his bottle off against his mouth
        (which he wipes with the back of his hand)
        and lift the knife again to peel an apple
        so carefully from stem to bud it is all

23

one red spiral, and toss it on a bush
to see it against green and color of loam
and slap the crumbs from his lap for the birds to have
before he sleeps with his hat over his eyes
(for a pillow he joins his hands behind his head)

that all the guns and lances looked to him
all the maps and marches centered here
and all the charges climbed this same small hill

that it was always this man in this field
through all of Europe and the island-South
the kingdoms and their kings were told about.

V

What the Roman sun says to the Romans
(a boy fishing the Tiber with a seine
while two old men and a tourist watch from the bridge
that leads to Castel Sant' Angelo, where once
a cypress forest mourned across the roof
for a faded emperor gone like his forest
into the stoneworks)
                              what the Roman sun
(a species of tumulus or burial mound
as for example pyramids cairns barrows
and similar monuments common to many cultures)
says to the Romans (the present structure
visible on the Tiber being simply the base)
I have said to you in all the tongues of sleep.

VI

The mountains quiver like a low flame
on the horizon. They flicker and reappear,
flicker and reappear. Sometimes
there are no mountains and sometimes
they are always there.
                              Mountains
have no need of being seen. They can outwait
all but these repetitions of the air.

The Invasion of Sleep Walkers
(What I shall say to my Father)

They were weeding out the dead at the funeral home
to reduce the overstock. Rack after rack
the wire-hung bones chattered their loneliness
and even the drunkenest angel wept and sang.
But the coroner's men were stuffed too full for hearing,
the trucks were backed to the wind, and the sleep walkers
already were pacing the streets, their eyes like spit,
their arms out stiff before them, their knees unbending,
their heels hitting too hard. They had no faces,
or, more exactly, they had the look of faces
that could not happen or that had not happened—
once on Fifth Avenue I watched two miles
of faceless cops march on St. Patrick's day
and learned that face forever—
                                There's not much more:
when the dead had been thinned out they put that face
over the skulls and gave them back to us.
We marched all day and night with flags and torches
to celebrate our thanks. The Great Good Face
stared down from photographs ten stories high.
It had no eyes but it saw my guilt at once
among a million marchers. I never learned
what signal passed between it and the Law,
but something certainly—and here I am.

Can Hell be taken more seriously than the world?

Temptation
> Volgiti indietro, e tien lo viso chiuso:
> chè, se il Gorgon si mostra, e tu il vedessi,
> nulla sarebbe del tornar mai suso.

St. Anthony, my father's holy man,
was tempted by a worm-shop, spills of guts,
soft coupling toads, blind fish, and seeing maggots.
The whores the devil sent leaked through their skin.

Now who would leave off heaven for such stuff?
What in the devil was the devil thinking
to try to turn a man with such a stinking
parcel of shoddy? Or were times so tough

he hadn't one small kingdom, or at least
one final Lilith to give sin some standing
a man could sell his soul for without branding
himself a damn fool before man and beast?

The devil's a better fisherman than angels
or he'd have starved long since. When slobs die poor
on rotten kingdoms and a nagging whore
still in her heat when every other chills,

the devil keeps that last bait for the ardent:
my father bit bare iron to go damned:
I see the leakage through the door he slammed:
I think the devil almost hooked his saint.

Addio

The corpse my mother made
panted all one afternoon
till her father called down, "Oh, stop that!"

I saw her hear and obey
and almost smile
to lie down good again.

Then that blinked gone.
She gaped, her face
a run wax she ran from.

I kissed her forehead and thought,
"It will never be warm again."
Oh, daughter, if *I* could call!

I MARRY YOU

To Judith Asleep

My dear, darkened in sleep, turned from the moon
That riots on curtain-stir with every breeze
Leaping in moths of light across your back . . . .
Far off, then soft and sudden as petals shower
Down from wired roses—silently, all at once—
You turn, abandoned and naked, all let down
In ferny streams of sleep and petaled thighs
Rippling into my flesh's buzzing garden.

Far and familiar your body's myth-map lights,
Traveled by moon and dapple. Sagas were curved
Like scimitars to your hips. The raiders' ships
All sailed to your one port. And watchfires burned
Your image on the hills. Sweetly you drown
Male centuries in your chiaroscuro tide
Of breast and breath. And all my memory's shores
You frighten perfectly, washed familiar and far.

Ritual wars have climbed your shadowed flank
Where bravos dreaming of fair women tore
Rock out of rock to have your cities down
In loot of hearths and trophies of desire.
And desert monks have fought your image back
In a hysteria of mad skeletons.
Bravo and monk (the heads and tails of love)
I stand, a spinning coin of wish and dread,

Counting our life, our chairs, our books and walls,
Our clock whose radium eye and insect voice
Owns all our light and shade, and your white shell
Spiraled in moonlight on the bed's white beach;
Thinking, I might press you to my ear
And all your coils fall out in sounds of surf
Washing away our chairs, our books and walls,
Our bed and wish, our ticking light and dark.

Child, child, and making legend of my wish
Fastened alive into your naked sprawl—
Stir once to stop my fear and miser's panic
That time shall have you last and legendry
Undress to old bones from its moon brocade.

Yet sleep and keep our prime of time alive
Before that death of legend. My dear of all

Saga and century, sleep in familiar-far.
Time still must tick *this is, I am, we are.*

Men Marry What They Need

Men marry what they need. I marry you,
morning by morning, day by day, night by night,
and every marriage makes this marriage new.

In the broken name of heaven, in the light
that shatters granite, by the spitting shore,
in air that leaps and wobbles like a kite,

I marry you from time and a great door
is shut and stays shut against wind, sea, stone,
sunburst, and heavenfall. And home once more

inside our walls of skin and struts of bone,
man-woman, woman-man, and each the other,
I marry you by all dark and all dawn

and have my laugh at death. Why should I bother
the flies about me? Let them buzz and do.
Men marry their queen, their daughter, or their mother

by hidden names, but that thin buzz whines through:
where reasons are no reason, cause is true.
Men marry what they need. I marry you.

Most Like an Arch This Marriage

Most like an arch—an entrance which upholds
and shores the stone-crush up the air like lace.
Mass made idea, and idea held in place.
A lock in time. Inside half-heaven unfolds.

Most like an arch—two weaknesses that lean
into a strength. Two fallings become firm.
Two joined abeyances become a term
naming the fact that teaches fact to mean.

Not quite that? Not much less. World as it is,
what's strong and separate falters. All I do
at piling stone on stone apart from you
is roofless around nothing. Till we kiss

I am no more than upright and unset.
It is by falling in and in we make
the all-bearing point, for one another's sake,
in faultless failing, raised by our own weight.

Morning: I Know Perfectly How in a Minute You Will Stretch and Smile

As pilots pay attention to the air
    lounging on triggers wired into their ease;
    seeing what they do not see, because their eyes
    are separate cells; hearing what they do not hear,
    because a life is listening in their place;
    and so with their five senses and a sixth
    cocked to their element, free and transfixed,
    slouch as they hurtle, ticking as they laze—

so in the mastered master element
    love is or nothing, silences unheard,
    flickerings unseen, and every balancing
    and tremor of our senses still unsensed,
    joins and enjoins, and, nothing left to chance,
    spins our precisions in us as we nod.

Censorship

Damn that celibate farm, that cracker-box house
with the bed springs screaming at every stir,
even to breathe. I swear, if one of us
half turned they'd shriek, "He's getting on top of her!"

Her father, but for the marriage certificate,
would have his .30—.30 up my ass.
Her mother, certificate or not, could hate
a hole right through the wall. It was

a banshee's way to primroses that fall
of the first year in that hate-bed wired
like a burglar alarm. If I stood her against the wall,
that would quiver and creak. When we got tired

of the dog-humped floor we sneaked out for a stroll
and tumbled it out under the apple tree
just up from the spring, but the chiggers ate us whole
in that locked conspiracy of chastity

whose belts we both wore all one grated week
while virtue buzzed a blue-fly over that bitch
of a bed hair-triggered to shriek:
"They're going at it! They're doing it right now!"—which

we damned well couldn't, welted over and on
as if we were sunburned. And every night at two
her mother would get up and go to the john,
and the plumbing would howl from Hell, "We're watching
     you!"

For Myra out of the Album

I changed the baby, fed it, dithered
and got dithered at, with a grin added
and arms and legs pumping,
which means "Hug me!" So I hugged
small as anything is done soft.

32

There was that hour once in a cone of light.

Outside the cone, the dithering universe.

I have been here, and some of it was love.

Boy

For Jonnel

He is in his room sulked shut. The small
pouts of his face clenched. His tears
as close to holy water as I recall
any first font shining. A boy, and fierce
in his sacrament, father-forced this two-
faced way love has. And I, who

am chain-chafed and galled as any son,
his jailor: my will, his cell;
his hot eyes, mine. "Whose will be done?"
I think, wrong as a man.—Oh, very well:
I make too much of nothing much. My
will a while. A boy's tears dry

into the smudge of any jam. Time hurts,
but I am not much destiny. I am,
at best, what cries with him; at worst,
a smallest God, the keeper of one lamb
that must be made to follow.—Where?
That takes more God than I am to make clear.

I'm wrong as a man is. But right as love,
and father of the man whose tears I bless
in this bud boy. May he have cried enough
when he has cried this little. I confess
I don't know my own reasons or own way.
May sons forgive the fathers they obey.

Saturday, March 6

One morning you step out, still in pajamas
to get your *Times* from the lawn where it lies folded
to the British pound, which has dropped below $2.00
for the first time since the sun stopped never
setting on it, and you pick it up—
the paper, that is—because it might mean something,
in which case someone ought to know about it
(a free and enlightened citizenry, for instance)
and there, just under it—white, purple, yellow—
are the first three crocuses half open, one
sheared off where the day hit it, and you pick it up,
and put it in water, and when your wife comes down
it's on the table. And that's what day it is.

Two Hours

I. EVENING

The low-fi scrapes the phrases from the strings
of something neither of us was listening to.
Whatever it is, the strings grate still, the drums
begin to cough a bronchial bass crack. You,
I, someone, thought a music, but it comes
wrong from the machine. Which brings

me to you-and-me as you start to undress
at last (which brings me to you) and how
frothily from foam-trim perkily your thighs
dimple and your arms reach and grow
till they are elements of the light and the wise
S's of your hips enter the great S
of your languor as, reaching behind,
you unstrap and unribbon and your breasts
go from the advertised to the invincible
first line of mantime, and a last rustle rests
you ungirdled at the bird-sung well
of gardens this twisted music cannot find,

of lights and airs and palpable here-and-now
to confound all Heaven's recorders and amplifiers.
How shall they hear us on any machine of theirs?
—your nakedness is more music than they have wires.
Yet, if it's true that angels watch in pairs,
they still may learn. Come here. We'll *show* them how.

II. MORNING

A morning of the life there is
in the house beginning again
its clutters in the sun

babbles and sways and tells
time from its sailing cribs. Enter
three pirate energies to murder sleep:

the bed rocks with their boarding:
a fusilade of blather
sweeps the white decks. We're taken!

—Good morning, sweet with chains.
We win all but the fight.
Do as they say—I'll meet you here tonight.

One Morning
for Benn

I remember my littlest one in a field
running so hard at the morning in him
he kicked the heads off daisies. Oh, wild
and windy and spilling over the brim
of his sun-up juices he ran
in the dew of himself. My son.

And the white flower heads
shot like sparks where his knees
pumped, and his hot-shod
feet took off from time, as who knows
when ever again a running morning will be
so light-struck, flower-sparked-full between him and me.

Three A.M. and Then Five

"Do you like your life?"
said the ghost of God-shadow
one wisp of a night blowing.

"You woke me to ask that?"
I growled through the phlegm of sleep.
"What else would wake you?" it said.

I wallowed in that wind forever,
the sheets a hair shirt,
practice-praying to no address.

Till my wife said, "Please lie still!"
So I went down into the wind
to where I had left the bourbon.

"No one knows me better," I told it.
"What do you think?"
"I may be too good for you," it said.

But it gentled, glowed, at last
whispered, "Go to sleep now."
I went back, the bed warm with her,

the sheets satin.
"Yes," I said to the ghost
yawningly, "Yes. Yes."

Tree Trimming

There's this to a good day's sweat
high in the branches trimming, and down
into the ground rooting—I'm not used to it
any more but it reminds me when I'm done
and sprawl shaky with tiredness, wet
in the sun's wringer. Sweat tells me again
who my people were. And yes, there's more
to it. But without sweat I wouldn't want
it. It takes the whole body to be sure

of what you're remembering. I can't
say my father's or my grandfather's name
a better way than this sog-tired numb
joy of having touched green growing
and the dirt under it and the day going.

Even then I can't really touch them. Not ever
again. They had first things and the power
and the ignorance that go to the receiver
of first things only; that and no more.

I've lost it. I'm my own first. There was never
a man of my blood before
who spoke more than one tongue, or *that*
in a way courts wouldn't laugh at.
My father did read some. But it was
his mountain he came from, not the mind
of man. He had ritual, not ideas. His
world that I cannot find
except as my body aches and sweats hewing,
was holy and dim. But doing
his work, I rest. I remember this:
it is good to be able. To hold axe and saw
and do first things again. I miss
this the desked days I go. I see
him here. I know him. But he is
more than I can teach my children. They
have no first life. *That* is their loss.
I wish we were Jews and could say
the names of what made us.
I could weep by slow waters for my son
who has no history, no name
he knows long, no ritual from which he came,
and no fathers but the forgotten.

He who could sweat down, tree by tree,
a whole wood and touch no memory.

THICKETS

Thoughts on Looking into a Thicket

The name of a fact: at home in that leafy world
chewed on by moths that look like leaves, like bark,
like owls, like death's heads; there, by eating flowers
and stones with eyes, in that zoo of second looks,
there is a spider, *phrynarachne d.*,
to whom a million or a billion years
in the humorless long gut of all the wood
have taught the art of mimicking a bird turd.

"It is on a leaf," writes Crompton, "that she weaves
an irregular round blotch, and, at the bottom,
a separate blob in faithful imitation
of the more liquid portion. She then squats
herself in the center, and (being unevenly marked
in black and white), supplies with her own body
the missing last perfection, *i.e.*, the darker
more solid central portion of the excreta."

Must I defend my prayers? I dream the world
at ease in its long miracle. I ponder the egg,
like a pin head in silk spit, invisibly stored
with the billion years of its learning. Have angels
more art than this? I read the rooty palm
of God for the great scarred Life Line. If you
'will be more proper than real, that is your
death. I think life will do anything for a living.

And that hungers are all one. So Forbes reports
that seeing a butterfly once poised on a dropping
he took it to be feasting, but came closer
and saw it was being feasted on. Still fluttering,
it worked its woolen breast for *phrynarachne*,
pumping her full. So once I saw a mantis
eating a grub while being itself eaten
by a copper beetle. So I believe the world

in its own act and accomplishment. I think
what feeds is food. And dream it in mosaic
for a Church of the First Passion: an ocher sea
and a life-line of blue fishes, the tail of each
chained into the mouth behind it. Thus, an emblem

of our indivisible three natures in one:
the food, the feeder, and the condition of being
in the perpetual waver of the sea.

I believe the world to praise it. I believe
the act in its own occurrence. As the dead
are hats and pants in aspic, as the red
bomb of the living heart ticks against time,
as the eye of all water opens and closes, changing
all that it has looked at—I believe
if there is an inch or the underside of an inch
for a life to grow on, a life will grow there;

if there are kisses, flies will lay their eggs
in the spent sleep of lovers; if there is time,
it will be long enough. And through all time,
the hand that strokes my darling slips to bone
like peeling off a glove; my body eats me
under the nose of God and Father and Mother.
I speak from thickets and from nebulae:
till their damnation feed them, all men starve.

Tommy's Pond

Frogs' eggs in globular clusters
cloud a jellied universe. A light-bending
Magellanic scum seeded with black lusters.
Has God said this sending?

In the pomegranate of Mother Church, saints
are such seed. Their ruby blood-beat—
cloud-bent, and again in the telling—taints
light as life does. It is no feat

to misunderstand a universe: all man-time
fables great possibility wrong.
Yet seed does burn. Slime
is a sure fire. Its puddle-hung

plenum will burst, these periods
become commas in a heartbeat beyond
pleroma, their myriad myriads
unsaid as galaxies. In any pond.

Fragment

To the laboratory then I went. What little
right men they were exactly! Magicians
of the microsecond precisely wired
to what they cared to ask no questions of
but such as their computers clicked and hummed.

It was a white-smocked, glass, and lighted Hell.
And their St. Particle the Septic sat
lost in his horn-rimmed thoughts. A gentlest pose.
But in the frame of one lens as I passed
I saw an ogre's eye leap from his face.

Differences

Choose your own difference between surgery
and knifing. Both cut. One
thinks to rejoin. Can something be made
of this difference? Defend your answer.

Now think of a surgery without intention:
here the scalpels, there the body.
Everyone is some doctor. You, too,
may as well be employed. Cut.

Is this something like a soft version
of a machine built to do nothing?
We are experimenting in the new art:
by contradicting purpose we explore,

possibly nothing, but explore,
possibly a reality, possibly a way

of inventing what a reality might be
had we some way of inventing it.

The first incision is hardest, but look
closely: you will find it already made,
inherent. Put the alarm clock inside it
and stitch. You now have a TV commercial

someone could be born to or die of.
And you? Are you my murderer
or my healer? You do know. Why else
did you set the alarm without being told?

Remember, however: distinctions
are never made wholly for their own sake.
You are doomed to decide not only
what you do but what you have done.

Yes, we chose what was already open,
putting into it what came to hand.
We must still take what attitude we can
toward what will already have been done

by the time we have time to think about it.
Were we successful killers or failed
surgeons? We will come to that difference.
And what difference will it make?

Sea Marshes in Winter

Marsh hummocks that were a sabbath hill
for a witches' dance of lives the last weather I looked,
go Christian as Calvary in the stone still
and sackcloth sky. At four, a wind-hooked
glacier of cloud chills a last thought and the snow
starts. And all that night that comes at once
the snow sifts dry as salt, scratching the window.
Then day leaks back from the edge. A half-light hunts
somewhere to settle, a place to begin, but slumps
onto the black-streaked sheet and the dead white humps
between me and the sea. It never quite—

44

not all that day—makes up to enough light
to see a world by. And still I look at this
world as worlds will be seen—in what light there is.

Gulls Land and Cease to Be

Spread back across the air, wings wide,
    legs out, the wind delicately
dumped in balance, the gulls ride
    down, down, hang, and exactly
touch, folding not quite at once
    into their gangling weight, but
taking one step, two, wings still askance,
    reluctantly, at last, shut,
        twitch one look around
        and are aground.

Birds, Like Thoughts

Watch a wild turkey come in to land—
(they are rare, but a man can find most
of what he wants if he wants it enough
to look for it)—you see a long slant
out of the air, like the approach of
some queer plane. Its landing gear first
let down, then agitated, it starts to run
before it touches, finishes yards on
from the point of touch down; and only then
folds its wings and is back, a hen again.

Not wrens, warblers, swallows—(I can't even see
what it is swallows do on the air. They
change it, exceed it, make it serve impossibility)—
all smaller (not lesser) birds play
instantly in and out of the air. There are no
parts to their coming, going. A whirl and they light;
a whirl, and they are airborne. Watch a jay go

its long dart through branches. It is too right
to need caution. It lands like an arrow
with no separation of its motions—So!

And there it is, and instantly gone if it feels
like it. Talk about landing on a dime!—
it could land on the edge of one. I've watched
every bird I could find to look at as it wheels,
heaves, whirls, glides. Whatever is hatched
to wings has its own way with them. But I'm
sure of one thing: the more weight you take to air,
the more space you need to get down
the more slowly. Birds are like thoughts: they're
more instant as they stay light. Both come and gone.

Bees and Morning Glories

Morning glories, pale as a mist drying,
fade from the heat of the day, but already
hunchback bees in pirate pants and with peg-leg
hooks have found and are boarding them.

This could do for the sack of the imaginary
fleet. The raiders loot the galleons even as they
one by one vanish and leave still real
only what has been snatched out of the spell.

I've never seen bees more purposeful except
when the hive is threatened. They know
the good of it must be grabbed and hauled
before the whole feast wisps off.

They swarm in light and, fast, dive in,
then drone out, slow, their pantaloons heavy
with gold and sunlight. The line of them,
like thin smoke, wafts over the hedge.

And back again to find the fleet gone.
Well, they got this day's good of it. Off
they cruise to what stays open longer.
Nothing green gives honey. And by now

you'd have to look twice to see more than green
where all those white sails trembled
when the world was misty and open
and the prize was there to be taken.

At First Flower of the Easy Day

At first flower of the easy day
a buck went wading through the mist.
Legless, he seemed to swim away.
A brown swan with a mythic twist
of antlers to his changeling head.
All that the weaving Greeks referred
to plastic nature's shifting thread

he evidenced. I saw him turn
and dip his head into that pond
and flash the white flag at his stern,
then lift his head and drift beyond
an isle of spruces to the right.
What do we ask of any wraith
but the Greek fact in its first light

that makes of morning's beasts the day
our nights would dream if they knew how?
Starting from this dawn, I could say
sad Io's name to any cow
and have her eyes confirm my guess.
Unless her farmer came like Zeus
and waved me off the premises.

The Size of Song

Some rule of birds kills off the song
in any that begin to grow
much larger than a fist or so.
What happens as they move along

to power and size? Something goes wrong.
Bird music is the tremolo
of the tremulous. Birds let us know
the songsters never are the strong.

One step more on the way of things,
we find a second rule applies
to birds that grow to such a size
they lose, or start to lose, their wings:
they start to lose the very strings
of sound itself. Give up the skies:
you're left your weight. And your last ties
to anything that sings.

An Aspect of the Air

Through my hemlocks and the spruce beyond,
mist hangs and closes. What change is this?
Not a bird dares it. Not so much as a frond
stirs in the shadowless absence
of this light I see by, not knowing what I see,
there in the green caves and up into a sky
that isn't there, except as there must be
some source for any light. I don't see, I
conjecture sources. It is too still
not to be thinking out from things, not to feel
a presence of the unreality that *will*
mystify what incloses us. Mist is not real;
not by the handful. And thought is not
fact, nor measurable. It is simply there.
An inclosing condition. A dimension taught
the sourceless light. An aspect of the air.

On Flunking a Nice Boy Out of School

I wish I could teach you how ugly
decency and humility can be when they are not
the election of a contained mind but only
the defenses of an incompetent. Were you taught
meekness as a weapon? Or did you discover,
by chance maybe, that it worked on mother
and was generally a good thing—
at least when all else failed—to get you over
the worst of what was coming. Is that why you bring
these sheepfaces to Tuesday?
                                    They won't do.
It's three months work I want, and I'd sooner have it
from the brassiest lumpkin in pimpledom, but have it,
than all these martyred repentances from you.

What Was Her Name?

Someone must make out the cards
for the funeral of the filing clerk.
Poor bony rack with her buzzard's
jowled eyes bare as a dirk
and as sharp for dead fact, she
could have done it better than anyone
will do it for her. It will be,
to be sure, done.
And the flowers sent. And the office closed
for the half day it takes
for whatever we are supposed
to make of the difference it makes
to file the filing clerk
where we can forget her.

Someone will do the work
she used to do better.

One Wet Iota

I could see God once when I believed telling
look into a mud and His eye
start one wet iota swelling.

An untold later toward some when and why
come to no answer, I put
a lesson to a lens and saw the jelly

webbed to bone-spars of a live frog's foot
flow like blips across a radar screen.
And that was all blood circling in and out.

Told or untold, I saw nothing mean
but small looking. I can look home
to the size God was, seeing the thing seen

start like that wet iota and become.

No White Bird Sings

Can white birds sing? An ornithologist
told me once there was a white bell bird
that rang whole tones, though only as separate notes.
"Is that singing?—sound without sequence?"
I said. "No, not exactly," he granted,
"but it is white." I granted him half a case.
This morning I heard a mockingbird again
and claimed my whole case back: no white bird sings.

I know some black poets who have been waiting
for just this image. So there it is, man:
an accident, but accidents are to use.
What else is a poem made of? Well, yes, ghosts.
But ghosts are only what accidents give birth to
once you have learned how to let accidents happen
purposefully enough to beget ghosts.

Bird song is itself an accident,
a code no different from wolf howl, warthog grunt,

porpoise twitter. It is a way of placing
the cardinal in its sconce, of calling its hen,
of warning off others. *That* code. We hear it
and *re*-code it: it sounds to us like something
we might like to try. Who cares how it sounds
to another bird? We take what we need from nature,
not what is there. We can only guess what is there.

Guess then: why does no white bird sing
to our pleasure? Because, I will guess, songsters
nest in green-dapple. There, what is white shines.
What shines is visible. What is most visible
is soonest hunted. What is soonest hunted
becomes extinct. To sing, one must hide in the world
one sings from, colored to its accidents
which are never entirely accidents. Not when one sings.

11:02 A.M. The Bird Disappeared

A humming bird darning the trumpet vine
pokes in, pokes out, pauses to look at the work.
What holds it up? Yes, wings—if this is a test
for the Civil Service and "wings" is one of the choices.
But shouldn't wings leave some blur? A hue—
as propellors darken a circle of air? This
leaves no trace. It is. And now it's gone.
And somewhere an Examiner shakes his head.

The Lung Fish
For SPOOF, The Society for the Preservation of Old Fish,
School of Fisheries, University of Washington

In Africa, when river beds
        crack, the lung fish
squirms into mud deeper than
        the two feet down of wrath, and

sleeps, its tail over its eyes
    to keep them from drying blind, its
snout at a blow-hole blueprinted
    in the egg, too small to read,

but read. No one, the lung fish least,
    knows how long it can wait. If no
creature is immortal, some
    are more stubborn than others.

If all sleep is a miracle, consider
    (through the poking lenses
of unraveling science) what
    miracle this is: The lung fish

digests its own tissues. Its wastes,
    which are normally an ammonia
safely dispersed in water, would
    in its cocoon, choke it. Therefore

it changes them to urea, which
    it can live with. Lung fish blood
is known to have six different
    hemoglobins—four more

than Moses took to God's desert.
    Like Moses, it has gone to legend
in Africa. It is said to be
    half fish, half croc. It is called

Kamongo there (but does not answer).
    If you cut off its head
(whether in fact or legend, and who
    knows which?) its jaws will snap

two days later. (Which
    we do know, all of us, about
what we cut off.) When
    Dr. Brown, an icthyologist

of Seattle, put Kamongo
    into a mud bottom aquarium
and lowered the water level, as God
    does at whim, this egg-born

instinctus of survival slept
        seventeen months. When it woke
in the reconfluence of time
        and whim, it seized stones with its mouth

and dinged them against the world's walls
        till it was fed—dinged them so hard
the doctor thought the walls might break
        between him and his creature. He drained it

back to sleep for time to build a world
        strong enough to hold both sleep
and waking. If anything can be. If we
        can learn sleep whole and not choke

on what we are while we learn it.

Two Egrets

On Easter morning two egrets
flew up the Shrewsbury River
between Highlands and Sea Bright

like two white hands
washing one another
in the prime of light.

Oh lemons and bells of light,
rails, rays, waterfalls, ices—
as high as the eye dizzies

into the whirled confetti
and rhinestones of the breaking blue
grain of lit heaven,

the white stroke of the egrets
turned the air—a prayer
and the idea of prayer.

Credibility

Who could believe an ant in theory?
a giraffe in blueprint?
Ten thousand doctors of what's possible
could reason half the jungle out of being.
I speak of love, and something more,
to say we are the thing that proves itself
not against reason, but impossibly true,
and therefore to teach reason reason.

One Jay at a Time

I have never seen a
generalized blue jay.
I have never heard a
specific one utter a
denial. Blue jays are
one at a time and they
are always screamers
of an assertion. Look
at that stiff dandy on
the sill-box. YES! YES!
YES! he screams forever
on a launching pad in-
side himself. I AM! I AM!
I AM! AND HERE I GO!

Come Morning

A young cock in his plebe strut
mounts the rail-fence to some
reviewing stand he has in mind
and practices commanding all those
blazed regiments eastward.

54

                              Not bad, boy!
Not quite full-toned, but willing.
You'll make it yet!
                        But suddenly
the damned Daddy-Colonel of them
all unfurls above our shavetail
like a flaming umbrella in a high
wind, and that's all brother! Our
lad's mustered out and running like
any civilian with hot hell on his tail.

Go it, boy! Old Jab-and-Spur has
blood in mind!
                        Till here comes
the Colonel back again strutting
posh as the dream of horse guards,
sets himself in place like Victoria's
best bustle, and, sucking a sky in,
lets go with the right high hot sound
for it, and makes it official. It's
morning!

Selectivity

Now mist takes the hemlocks and nothing
stirs. This is a gray-green and a
glassy thing and nothing stirs. A plane
to or from Newark burrs down idling on
its flaps or grinds full-rich up its
airy grade, and I hear it. Mrs. Levy calls
her kids and I hear her. A train eight
blocks away rolls and I hear it. And
tire sounds. And a car door closing
dully. And a whole helluva caterwaul
when Richard hits Benn again and Benn does
stir. He comes running. And I hear it.
And then the phone rings and, carefully,
I do not hear it. I am listening selectively.

My Tribe

Everyone in my tribe hates
everyone in your tribe.

Every girl in my tribe wants to
be there when we bring in anyone
from your tribe. Our girls save faggots
in their hope chests for you.

Every boy in my tribe has a peg
from which to hang the scalp of
anyone in your tribe. Our boys
hone knives in their dreams of you.

Everyone in my tribe is proud of
our boys and their dreams, of our
girls and their trousseaus. Our lives
have dear goals across which we

shall all finally kick all of your
heads. We are united.

Fast As You Can Count to Ten

Fast as you can count to ten
commandments, I would count to
twenty forgivenesses, could I
think which twenty, and till I
can, let me offer all and with-
out number and beg for myself,
if you please, your used mercies.

Song for an Allegorical Play

Ah could we wake in mercy's name—
the church mouse in each other's eyes
forgiven, the warthog washed in flame

56

confessed—when paunch from paunch we rise,
false and unmartyred, to pretend
we dress for Heaven in the end.

To look and not to look away
from what we see, but, kindly known,
admit our scraping small decay
and the gross jowls of flesh on bone—
think what a sweetness tears might be
in mercy, each by each set free.

Only Success is beast enough
to stop our hearts. Oh twist his tail
and let him howl. When best we love
we have no reason but to fail,
in reason learning as we live
we cannot fail what we forgive.

That mouse is in your eyes and mine.
That warthog wallows in our blood.
But, ah, let mercy be our sign,
and all our queer beasts, understood,
shall rise, grown admirable, and be,
in mercy, each by each set free.

Goodnight

An oyster that went to bed x-million years ago,
tucked itself into a sand-bottom, yawned (so to speak),
and woke high in the Grand Canyon of the Colorado.

If I am not here for breakfast, geologize at will.

Fragment of a Bas Relief

The knife, the priest, the heifer
Wander stonily into shadows of erosion,
Profiles of gem-eyed Egypt.

How shall I ever believe the world is real?

In Place of a Curse

At the next vacancy for God, if I am elected,
I shall forgive last the delicately wounded
who, having been slugged no harder than anyone else,
never got up again, neither to fight back,
nor to finger their jaws in painful admiration.

They who are wholly broken, and they in whom
mercy is understanding, I shall embrace at once
and lead to pillows in heaven. But they who are
the meek by trade, baiting the best of their betters
with the extortions of a mock-helplessness

I shall take last to love, and never wholly.
Let them all into Heaven—I abolish Hell—
but let it be read over them as they enter:
"Beware the calculations of the meek, who gambled nothing,
gave nothing, and could never receive enough."

The One Dull Thing You Did Was to Die, Fletcher
for Fletcher Pratt

To you, Fletcher, from my dark house asleep
in the sound of its lives breathing, at three
of a tired morning, and, as it happens,
in Rome—which could be Oslo or Shanghai
to any sense of mine: a place like any,
a distance equally anywhere from you
engraved in your dull death—and a damn poor likeness . . . .

58

I read a fool's book late, then puttered
along a marble hall a block long nowhere
at a hundred-thousand lire a month, and poured
my last shot of real Armagnac.
                                And now,
here I stand, a sheep-face in the mirror,
the drink raised in this crazy Italian dim
of every bulb too small for what it does
and everyone saving a lira the wrong way.

Here I stand in this light that sticks to shadow
without half changing it, and there you are
as long as rent, and time wherever *it* is
in a lira's worth of something saved from dying.
God, what a silly way to keep a budget!
. Well, here goes: from your budget's end and mine,
the last of what there is—to you, Fletcher,
maudlin, but in the best that money can buy.

Annals

Tricodon of Bruges, a Flemish
Poet of no reputation and
Of no talent but tears,
Wept into his inkwell
All one night, then hanged himself—
His only gift to the dawn.

Aldo, the tragedian of Padua,
Was another weeper. Passion in him
Invited all accident. Sandbags
Rained on his love scenes, flies
Wavered on his battles, the doors of his castles
Fell on him when he bolted them.

Malorca of Galicia was another.
A defender. Shot at his wife's lover
And killed the General's palomino.
He left his tears on a wall in Estremadura:

God grant me sustenance within myself
To bear the dirty chuckle of the wind.

Sophia of Montenegro died naked in a pie
On her way to the Duke's table. Her own
Golden surprise for him. But he
Was dining in his chambers with La Guernerra
When his firebird sank through its gilding
Under the lorgnette of the Countess Merla.

Otto, the declaimer at the court of Saxony,
Swore to the Elector on his head
There were no Poles at Frieden
That two dogs and one huntsman could not take.
Smerzni, who felled him, sent the head to court:
I hear, my cousin, your general owes you this.

To remember what has never been is not
To lie but to read the future:
A place in nature where Polonius the pincushion
Stitched into a tapestry of Clichy
Speaks into Van Gogh's ear, and all perceive
The action of incorrigible farce.

Faces

Once in Canandaigua, hitchhiking from Ann Arbor
to Boston in the middle of December, and just
as dark came full on a stone-cracking
drill of wind that shot a grit of snow,
I was picked up outside an all-night diner
by a voice in a Buick. "Jump in," it said. "It's cold."

Four, five miles out, in the dead winter of nowhere
and black as the insides of a pig, we stopped.
"I turn off here."

          I looked around at nothing.
"The drive's up there," he said.

                    But when I was out,
he headed on, turned round, drove back, and stopped.
"You haven't thanked me for the ride," he said.

60

"Thanks," I said, shuffling to find a rock
I might kick loose and grab for just in case.
But he wasn't that kind of crazy. He just waved:
"You're welcome, brother. Keep the rest for change."
Then he pulled in his head and drove away—
back toward Canandaigua.

                    I thought about him
a good deal, you might say, out there in the sandblast
till a truck lit like a liner picked me up
one blue-black inch from frostbite.
And off and on for something like twenty years
I've found him in my mind, whoever he was,
whoever he is—I never saw his face,
only its shadow—but for twenty years
I've been finding faces that might do for his.
The Army was especially full of possibles,
but not to the point of monopoly. Any party
can spring one through a doorway. "How do you do?"
you say and the face opens and there you are
back in the winter blast.

                    But why tell you?
It's anybody's world for the living in it:
You know as much about that face as I do.

Divorced, Husband Demolishes House
    —News Item

It is time to break a house.
What shall I say to you
but torn tin and the shriek
of nails pulled orange
from the ridge pole? Rip it
and throw it away. Beam
by beam. Sill, step, and lintel.
Crack it and knock it down.
Brick by brick. (I breathe
the dust of openings. My tongue
is thick with plaster. What can I
say to you? The sky has come

through our rafters. Our windows
are flung wide and the wind's
here. There are no doors
in or out.) Tug it
and let it crash. Haul it.
Bulldoze it over. What can I say
to you except that nothing
must be left of the nothing
I cannot say to you? It's
done with. Let it come down.

Joshua on Eighth Avenue

A man can survive anything except not caring
and even that's not mortal enough
to stop his drinking, except of course
that even drinking can be a kind of
                                    caring.

Sometimes it takes a kind of at least
heroism to look entirely at Eighth Avenue
without anesthetic. Where would a man
get the sort of courage that risks
                                    pity?

Frontiersmen maybe. Those whiskery hermits
that had to prove themselves to every
bear and redskin. But those were haters.
Which of them had the courage to risk a
                                    tear?

Not anyhow Joshua, the old rumpot. He's
not daring anything sober, least of all
the question. Assuming there's one left
in him. What question? You crazy? This is
                                    Joshua

you're talking about. "Hey, Mac," he says,
"buy a ticket to my funeral. Ringside

for one drink. Or sell you my left leg
for a pint. Going out of business. Everything must be
                    sold.

Whattayasay? Everybody needs a funeral
to go to."—And so for the third time
this year I buy his left leg. And once more own
more pieces than I can put to one
                    man.

The Bird in Whatever Name

A bird with a name it does not itself
recognize, and I cannot recall—
if ever I knew it, and no matter—
lives off the great gross Rhinoceros of Africa.

The slathering hide of the great gross Rhinoceros,
slabbed like a river in a stiff wind,
is rancid at the bent seams, and clogged
with lice and fly-grubs at the pores and pittings.

The Rhino-bird, whatever its unknown name,
attends its warty barge through the jungle,
the feast of its own need picking the tickle
of many small corruptions from behemoth,

who, impervious to all roarers, is yet defenseless, alone,
against the whine of the fly in his ear, and stricken
to helpless furies by the squirm of the uncoiling grub
tucked into the soft creases of the impenetrable.

My bird—and oh it is my bird and yours!—crawls
him as kissingly as saints their god, springs
circling over him to foretell all coming,
descends in the calm lapses to ride a-perch on his horn

or snout. Even into the mouth and nares of the beast
he goes—so some have reported—to pick infection
from power. And can the beast not love
the bird that comes to him with songs and mercies?

—Oh jungle, jungle, in whose ferns life dreamed itself
and woke, saw itself and was, looked back
and found in every bird and beast its feature,
told of itself, whatever name is given.

A Thousandth Poem for Dylan Thomas

Waking outside his Babylonian binge
    in the wet and cramp of morningstone, the sot
begins his daily death. A first stiff wince
    numbers his bones, each like a tooth of God.

Where did night end? Girlies in a red flame
    squeal through his broken memory like pigs:
Hell's barnyard burning or the zoo of days,
    stampeded shapes exploded from their skins.

He tastes again the ooze of a first sigh
    dead in his throat; his mouth, a rotten fig;
his sex, a broken glue-pot in the thighs;
    his breath, a shudder from below the will.

Sooner or later he must break an eye
    to look at what he sees of what he is.
An angel beating at the trap of time?
    A bird-heart pulsing in an idiot's fist?

Both. Either. Floated open from its muds,
    that moment in the clear, the sot's eye sees
as much as saints could bear of the fireblood
    God's heart pumps in its seizure of the skies.

Then how the man could sing his ghost to tears,
    there in God's eye and blood, for that lost place
where he was innocent, before his need
    changed to a thirst inside the worm of waste.

He pours his celebrations of regret,
    tormented joyous from the throat of mud,
hawk-hearted as Augustine in his sweat,
    dove-eyed as Francis' bridal with the wood.

64

It is the age of sots. Our holiness
    wakens outside the minareted fronts
of a jazzy, airless, and expensive hell.
    He sings our wish. He drinks his death for us

who have no throats to die of or to sing.
    He is Saint Binge at death in his own meat,
the blaze meant in the char we make of things,
    our addict, and our angel of defeat.

Was a Man

Ted Roethke was a tearing man,
    a slam-bang wham-damn tantrum O
from Saginaw in Michigan
    where the ladies sneeze at ten below
but any man that's half a man
    can keep a sweat up till the freeze
    gets down to ninety-nine degrees.
    For the hair on their chests it hangs down to their knees
    in Saginaw, in Michigan.

Ted Roethke was a drinking man,
    a brandy and a bubbly O.
He wore a roll of fat that ran
    six times around his belly O,
then tucked back in where it began.
    And every ounce of every pound
    of that great lard was built around
    the very best hooch that could be found
    in Saginaw, in Michigan.

Ted Roethke was an ath-a-lete.
    (So it's pronounced in Michigan.)
He played to win and was hard to beat.
    And he'd scream like an orangutan
and claw the air and stamp his feet
    at every shot he couldn't make
    and every point he couldn't take.

And when he lost he'd hold a wake,
    or damn you for a cheat.

Sometimes he was a friend of mine
    with the empties on the floor O.
And, God, it's fun to be feeling fine
    and to pour and pour and pour O.
But just to show we were not swine
        we kept a clock that was stopped at ten,
        and never started before then.
        And just to prove we were gentlemen
        we quit when it got to nine.

Ted Roethke was a roaring man,
    a ring-tailed whing-ding yippee O.
He could outyell all Michigan
    and half the Mississippi O.
But once he sat still and began
        to listen for the lifting word,
        it hovered round him like a bird.
        And oh, sweet Christ, the things he heard
        in Saginaw, in Michigan!

Now Roethke's dead. If there's a man,
    a waking lost and wanting O,
in Saginaw, in Michigan,
    he could hear all his haunting O
in the same wind where it began
        the terrors it could not outface,
        but found the words of, and by grace
        of what words are, found time and place
        in Saginaw, in Michigan.

A Crate of Sterling Loving Cups

I had gone to a freightyard auction of sealed crates.
Like parenthood, you bid, then see what you've got.
Mine opened to an idea: I was sure I knew
enough beautiful people to give them out to.

The engraving couldn't cost much: *This cup is presented*
to X-X-X from our shared transience
in recognition of at least one moment
in which the donor thought YOU ARE BEAUTIFUL.

I had the first in mind for Archie MacLeish.
I'd have to come down a notch to find a second,
but the precedent would be set. To qualify
one would have, by God, to qualify. What are we

if we can't choose example?—A local fool
printed the story with application forms.
As if one could apply to be beautiful.
In a sense, I suppose, one must, but supporting letters,

especially from one's mother, do not count.
Nor fair employment practices. Nor guide-lines
from the grinning presidency. Nor minority pickets
blatting definition from a bullhorn.

I have nothing to say to this mindless generation
that thinks to be chosen rare by filling blanks
in my fool neighbor's forms. This mail is his.
I dump the daily basketful at his door

and burn what he returns to me. Soon now
I shall be leaving for Key West for the winter.
My house there is un-numbered, my phone unlisted.
It will do no good to try me as OCCUPANT:

you won't have found me till I answer, and I
shall be busy reading. The contest is called off.
(I'm sorry, Archie. New postal regulations
forbid the mailing of anything real and accurate.)

When I get back I shall have them melted down—
or hammered, or whatever it is one does—
into something useful. I'd like a large tureen
with a matching ladle. I do make a good soup.

What's left could make bowls enough and spoons enough
to set a table for a trial guest list.
Or even for a more-or-less open house.
Soup is a good that doesn't invite ambition.

ON THE PATIO

On the Patio

The rose at the edge of my tax structure
    sways in the breeze before twilight.
Ribbons of a scent that snares me
    whorl from it. I imagine I see them.
Like spirals flowing from Venetian glass.
    It is an air like glass I sit to.
Need it be real to be real enough?
    How real are angels?—yet Vaticans
have bedrocked on an air they stirred. As I
    have ground my hands black, even bled a little,
to turn a fantasy of a sort: the bed
    is weeded, pruned, mulched, watered.
I have paid the taxes on it. Roses
    are not for nothing. I have done
what pleased me painfully. Now I sit
    happy to look at what I look at.

When has a rose been looked at enough?
    A petal can be a shell of lemon
marked at the hinges like a pitted peach
    thumbed open warm from the tree,
but veined paler. What an intricate
    precision it takes to call a bee,
another and another intricacy veining
    to the heart of the rose—the "yellow"
as Dante knew it before hybridizers
    stained some strains red to the core
(though pinks and whites still wash to a yellow center).
    In being intricate nature is pliable.
By growing intricate enough I may yet
    come to see what I look at.
It is not easy. It is better than easy:
    it is joyously difficult. It is never
what one expected before looking. Tomorrow
    I must spray for aphids before they come,
and pay the Lawn Shop something on account.

Are accounts an offense to nature? With my hand
    I can reach six inches into the soil of that bed.

That is not nature, but makes roses. By frost time
    the tree rose must be burlapped and laid flat,
half its roots folded, the other half let loose,
    then buried again in moss and old compost,
hay, if I can find it (which I doubt),
    and then more burlap (which I have not yet paid for).
But the grafts have taken. They should bear next year
    four-colored from one stem. If that,
as I believe, is a loveliness, and not
    mere ingenuity of contrivance
(which it is, of course, but still lovely)
    it is budgeted for a grafting knife, tape, wax,
cans of Miracle-Gro, a sprayer, sprays.
    Add what the root stock cost me: a time ago
I ate for a semester on something less
    than a rose comes to. Not that price matters.
Until you haven't got it. I still have,
    and note it to pay gladly for what I buy,
wanting it more than what I spend.
    As I read catalogues for their complications.
It is not simplicity I am waiting to see
    but the rose that will not come easy
and must be painstaken beyond nature.

Suburban

Yesterday Mrs. Friar phoned. "Mr. Ciardi,
    how do you do?" she said. "I am sorry to say
this isn't exactly a social call. The fact is
    your dog has just deposited—forgive me—
a large repulsive object in my petunias."

I thought to ask, "Have you checked the rectal grooving
    for a positive I.D.?" My dog, as it happened,
was in Vermont with my son, who had gone fishing—
    if that's what one does with a girl, two cases of beer,
and a borrowed camper. I guessed I'd get no trout.

But why lose out on organic gold for a wise crack?
"Yes, Mrs. Friar," I said, "I understand."
"Most kind of you," she said. "Not at all," I said.
I went with a spade. She pointed, looking away.
"I always have loved dogs," she said, "but really!"

I scooped it up and bowed. "The animal of it.
I hope this hasn't upset you, Mrs. Friar."
"Not really," she said, "but really!" I bore the turd
across the line to my own petunias
and buried it till the glorious resurrection

when even these suburbs shall give up their dead.

Knowing Bitches

I was spading a flower bed while the old dog
inspected the lawn for memories of rabbits.
We used to have them till he hunted them out.

He walks the way I spade: it gets done
if there isn't much to do, but keeps pausing
to look back, or to look at anything.

I hadn't been listening to the bitch next door.
Her rave had become a background noise. It changed.
She had wormed under the fence and was coming mean

and meaning to be heard. I threw a clod
that spun her into circles. One of them
cut twice through my peonies. I gave a shout.

Ponti and his boys came running and shouting.
My boys came running and shouting. It would have done
for a race riot: *death to peonies!*

—Except for the old dog. He went on sniffing.
People and bitches are noisy but the earth's
to sniff and think about. When she broke through

he didn't even look up till she tried a nip.
Then, with no parts to his motion, he knocked her over
and stood astride her belly, his jaws at her throat,

not biting, then walked away stiff-legged
while she crawled after, belly to the grass,
till Ponti caught her collar and hauled her back

ravening at the leash. We waved "that's that."
I finished spading and sat on the patio.
The old dog finished sniffing and sprawled by me.

The boys found something else to shout about.
With luck and staking the peonies might come through.
The thing about bitches is knowing who *you* are.

Craft

A cherry red chrome dazzle
with white racing stripes
screams into my drive spilling
hard-rock enough to storm Heaven,
and young insolence sits there
honking for Benn, who's not in.

I put down my book
and press the crafty button
that works the black paint spray,
and press the crafty button
that jabs spikes through the drive
into all four wheels at once,

and press the crafty button
that blows his radio circuits.
Then move the crafty lever
that works the axle snips.
I am happy in my craft;
glad to learn ways to live.

Why does the blare not stop?
He does stop honking.

He slams into the house:
"Couldn't you hear me?"
"I have tried not to," I say, "is that
your radio or the fire siren?"

He beams. "Great sound, huh?"
Then: "Where's Benn?" "In earshot,"
I tell him. "Everything must be."
"Well, is he here or not?"
"He left for Boston this morning."
"Boston, huh? Well, tell him I was here."

"He knows," I say. "It's only
two hundred and fifty miles.
That's within earshot."
"Huh?" he says, wrinkling his nose.
I press my last craftiest button,
but the servo-genie

has shorted out. The trap door
does not open. There is no oil
in the kettle under the floor
and it is not boiling. He does
leave—in a four wheel drift
that smokes the turn-around—

without killing himself,
nor skidding into my arbor again.
That's as near a good as craft
could have worked it. It takes none
to know he'll work it out himself
some loud night on the Interstate.

Between

I threw a stick. The dog
ran to fetch, but dropped it
and began to dig, right there
in mid-lawn, clawing up
four half-curled baby rabbits

the size of Italian sausage,
two gulps apiece to him. Then
found the stick and fetched,
and I threw, and he fetched.

A Poem for Benn's Graduation from High School

Whenever I have an appointment to see the assistant
principal about my son again, if they will keep
him (which no one wants to and sometimes I)
it is always at 9:00 impossible o'clock A.M.

It is at least twenty years since I made it to
9:00 unbearable o'clock A.M. from the south side of sleep.
My one way there is the polar route over the Late Late
hump of the swozzled world's chain-smoking fog.

I do not seek these differences between me and
assistant whomevers. I am confined to them. Bit
by bit the original wiring of my nervous system
has been converted to solid state insomnia.

It does no good now to reverse the leads or to try
reprinting the circuits. At 9:00 paralyzed o'clock
A.M., in the name of what can despair and still
attend, I nod to the repetitions of the assistant

whomness. We are both dull as the Mudville choir
flatting platitudes. I could by now have been drunk,
enough possibly to doze. I do not need
to be stoned sleepless to know this boy is

difficult but more possible than this assistant
who-bah brisking me to ideal endeavor, community
cooperation, and the general detritus of the white
man's burden after the wreck of the Hesperus and

the spread of the Dutch Elm Beetle, which floated
ashore in logs ordered to be the ridge beams of
Wiley's Cozy Corner Sunset Rest Motel (local
residents only after previous identification)—

or as the bus driver between Victoria and Russell
(Kansas) ritualized at the end of the line:
"Last stop. Kindly let all those going out first."
(I have been free-associating past the assistant whom

and the blanks thereof. I might as well have been
inhaling Richard M. Nixon, the elephant's
capo dei capi, or some other maunder.) My son
is bored incommunicado. I am drafted to boredom

and must answer by name, rank, and serial number. It
ends. He, still sinus-smelling last night's pot,
goes off to his American-Dream-and-After
Seminar. I go for two eggs-up with bacon at Joe's,

garden for two hours, stir and reject the mail, and
doze off just in time for the 4:30 P.M. Great-Great-
Master-Marvel-Universal-Premiere (no Reruns ever)
Movie, which is all about carefully covered crotches.

When I wake to the trembling of the last, symbolized,
plagiarized, living-color veil, I find my son half
asleep in the other polar route chair to 9:00 inedible
o'clock A.M. "Well?" I say. "Hello, you old bastard,"

he says. So ends the trial of all assistant
whomnesses. Ours is no summary justice. We have
deliberated and found them guilty of being
exactly themselves. It does not, finally,

take much saying. There has even been time
to imagine we have said "Goddamn it, I love you,"
and to hear ourselves saying it, and to pause
to be terrified by *that* thought and its possibilities.

Encounter

"We," said my young radical neighbor, smashing my window,
"speak the essential conscience of mankind."

"If it comes to no more than small breakage," I said, "speak
away.

But tell me, isn't smashing some fun for its own sake?"

"We will not be dismissed as frivolous," he said,
grabbing my crowbar and starting to climb to the roof.

"You are seriously taken," I said, raising my shotgun.
"Please weigh seriously how close the range is."

"Fascist!" he said, climbing down. "Or are you a liberal
trying to fake me with no shells in that thing?"

"I'm a lamb at windows, a lion on roofs," I told him.
"You'll more or less have to guess for yourself what's loaded

until you decide to call what may be a bluff.
Meanwhile, you are also my neighbor's son:

if you'll drop that crowbar and help me pick up this glass,
I could squeeze a ham-on-rye from my tax structure,

and coffee to wash it down while we sit and talk
about my need of windows and yours to smash them."

"Not with a lumpen-liberal pseudo-fascist!"
he sneered, and jumped the fence to his own yard.

There's that about essential consciences:
given young legs, they have no trouble at fences.

The Catalpa

The catalpa's white week is ending there
in its corner of my yard. It has its arms full
of its own flowering now, but the least air
spins off a petal and a breeze lets fall
whole coronations. There is not much more
of what this is. Is every gladness quick?
That tree's a nuisance, really. Long before
the summer's out, its beans, long as a stick,
will start to shed. And every year one limb
cracks without falling off and hangs there dead
till I get up and risk my neck to trim
what it knows how to lose but not to shed.

78

I keep it only for this one white pass.
The end of June's its garden; July, its Fall;
all else, the world remembering what it was
in the seven days of its visible miracle.

What should I keep if averages were all?

Keeping

Put a dog in a bottle. It won't bark.
Not long. A scuba diver can't. He'll
swim up to the cork and try knifing it.
He has about thirty minutes to knife through.
Sometimes, for the strongest, that's enough.
If, therefore, you really mean
to keep things bottled, do not fill to the top.
It may be better to use no liquids at all.
Some ferment and blow the cork.
Any of them makes the bottle heavy
and the act of bottling up is itself
heavy enough. Suppose you were to spend
all your nights for years building a ghost ship
or a replica of your nervous system
inside the bottle, then filled it with water:
unless you used some nonbiodegradable
plastic junk, the thing would waterlog
and turn to bloat. If it didn't disintegrate
it would run, leaving you a dirty bottle.
It is a nuisance enough to carry the thing around
without having to watch it go dirty.
Not that you can manage without one.
You have yours. I have mine. We all
have something to put into it. Does it matter
what? We aren't given much choice.
Often, as I sense it, we have nothing to do
with actually doing it. We look,
and there is the bottle with things in it—
the dog, for example, that stopped barking

instantly its forty years ago
but starts again unstopped the instant we look
and remember there is the bottle, and what's in it.

Requisitioning
I needed 800 dozen golf balls.
I got 1700 basketball hoops.
—From an advertisement by Western Electric

There are no imperfect answers from perfect data.

Spec numbers, state of Inventory-Now,
urgency of requirement as crosshatched
from orders outstanding, credit substantiation,
promised delivery plus days of grace,
seasonal-demand configuration
adjusted for such variables as weather,
shifts in population, inductive events
(the sales effect, for example, of opening day
of the baseball season), duration of induction,
disposable income, demographic doctrine
—all must be weighed where all things balance true.

The answers are beyond us, not the method.
We describe our need, submitting it as we know it,
laboring always for the perfected input.

The Circuits then decide. We may think, at first,
they ignore our need. In time we understand
they scan that total universe of data
that is not visible to us at our stations.

We think we need 800 dozen golf balls:
good faith has been tendered, the customer confirmed,
we get back 1700 basketball hoops
and the customer phones for redemption: rains
have flooded the courses, the play has moved indoors,
gyms are under construction everywhere:
the need is for 3000 basketball hoops
with nets, backboards, brackets.

80

We absolve him
and send up the conversion. We get back
5000 pairs of water skis—regular, slalom,
trick, a few with hydroplanes.—Of course!
the flooding has been calculated. Seepage
has warped the gym floors. Cancel basketball.

We learn to answer as we are willed to answer
where all our needs are known before we know them
and ministered to our good.

There are, to be sure,
those 1700 basketball hoops, now surplus,
but before we can remainder them, Public Works
sends in an order for them as mooring rings.

That, too, as we see backwards, was foreseen.

There in the total universe of data
all things are parts and harmonies of one plan
that calls us to Itself, demanding only
our faith and our vocation to describe
fallibly, but laboring for perfection,
the need that shall be given perfect answers.

In the Hole

I had time and a shovel. I began to dig.
There is always something a man can use a hole for.
Everyone on the street stopped by. My neighbors
are purposeful about the holes in their lives.
All of them wanted to know what mine was *for*.

Briggs asked me at ten when it was for the smell
of new-turned sod. Ponti asked at eleven
when it was for the sweat I was working up.
Billy LaDue came by from school at one
when it was for the fishing worms he harvested.

My wife sniffed in from the Protestant ethic at four
when the hole was for finding out if I could make

a yard an hour. A little after five
a squad car stopped and Brewster Diffenbach,
pink and ridiculous in his policeman suit,

asked if I had a building permit. I told him
to run along till he saw me building something.
He told me I wasn't being cooperative.
I thanked him for noticing. I invited him
to try holding his breath till he saw me change.

I ate dinner sitting on its edge. My wife
sniffed it out to me and sniffed away.
She has her ways but qualifies—how shall I say?—
alternatively. I'd make it up to her later.
At the moment I had caught the rhythm of digging.

I rigged lights and went on with it. It smelled
like the cellar of the dew factory. Astonishing
how much sky good soil swallows. By ten-thirty
I was thinking of making a bed of boughs at the bottom
and sleeping there. I think I might have wakened

as whatever I had really meant to be once.
I could have slept that close to it. But my wife
came out to say NOTHING WHATEVER, so I showered
and slept at her side after making it up to her
as best I could, and not at all bad either.

By morning the hole had shut. It had even
sodded itself over. I suspect my neighbors.
I suspect Diffenbach and law and order.
I suspect most purposes and everyone's
forever insistence I keep mine explainable.

I wish now I had slept in my hole when I had it.
I would have made it up to my wife later.
Had I climbed out as I had meant to be—
really meant to be—I might have really
made it up to her. I might have unsniffed her

clear back to dew line, back to how it was
when the earth opened by itself and we
were bared roots.—Well, I'd had the exercise.

God knows I needed it and the ache after
to sing my body to sleep where I remembered.

And there *was* a purpose. This is my last house.
If all goes well, it's here I mean to die.
I want to know what's under it. One foot more
might have hit stone and stopped me, but I doubt it.
Sand from an old sea bottom is more likely.

Or my fossil father. Or a mud rosary.
Or the eyes of the dog I buried south of Jerusalem
to hide its bones from the Romans. Purpose
is what a man uncovers by digging for it.
Forgive me my neighbors. Forgive me Brewster Diffenbach.

To a Lovely Lady Gone to Theory

You could be the beginning of treated birds
that have changed their migration patterns.

Doctor Tinker has found the code written
on the inner wall of the egg and transcribed it.

Now he can read it, but the birds can't.
Some of them start south again every Tuesday.

When I come home too fast then, my scrambler
jamming the State Police radar,

they hear my wavelength as a mating signal
and light on my roof, drunk with a wrong nisus.

You wouldn't entirely believe what happens
in the jungle gym of my TV antenna.

Then, in a week, the weighted egg yet to come,
their new signal scrambles them south again.

Some of them. Many, I know, do not make it.
Some no longer balance on the air.

I find bodies in the driveway. Or my mower
sprays them. I no longer drive on Tuesdays

for fear of calling them or the State Cops.
I depend on cabs and on having nowhere to go.

On Wednesday, when I find you there, we are both
littered with dead birds. Is there no end to them?

They keep on coming faster than they die.
Then they keep dying almost as fast as they come.

Sometimes they sing as if all were well again.
I am tempted to doubt what I know about them. And us.

Always then it comes Tuesday again and it starts;
Wednesday, and once more I know what I know.

Sooner or later, I see, I must give you up
to that tireless Doctor who meddles with everything.

Go to him: finish building your faith around him.
I have had enough of watching us go random,

everything responding but in no sequence.

On the Orthodoxy and Creed of My Power Mower

All summer in power, outroaring the bull fiend,
    it raves on my lawn, spewing
  into the dirty lung hung on its side.
    Myself maddened by power, I ride
the howl of hot new-mown sacks-full,
    the powder bursts of gnashed mole runs,
till in one sweaty half day of the beast
    my lawn is lined to tidy passages. So
neatness from lunacy, the orderliness of rage,
    Bedlam's Eden, all calm now,
the dead beast washed in cool light and stalled.

Again and again, all summer in power at a touch,
    it frenzies. At fall's dry last
  I kneel to the manual, to the word, touch,
    and pour extreme unctions that the locked life
waken when called. And do call, year after year

84

in season, to the lunacy of power and am not answered.
I probe, prime, pump, and might as well pray
   to headless stone gods. Nothing—
nothing I know—wakens the power blast
   hidden in it, which is no cause of protestant
conscience to be worked out between me and the source
   but a priest-held power of maintenance.

Always at last defeated, I call, and its priest comes
   with cups, knowledge, and the anointed touch
that does reach power and mystery. The beast
   gasps, shakes, wavers deep in itself, then
roars full to resurrection, and here we come
   to cure green again, our triumph of faith!
Which is, of course, that even the powerless
   and inept may ride fit power once wakened
by the anointed man believed in
   deeper than conscience and defeat;
whole in his knowledge given, his touch charged,
   the dangerous blind beast tame in service.

A Prayer to the Mountain

Of the electric guitar as a percussion instrument
and of my son who wails twelve hours an animal day
in the stoned cellar of my house I sing, oh pothead baby
from the rock rolled Nine Sisters classic crag group
hit album featuring The Body Counts in "I'm Blowing it Now"
from "Don't Have to Have a Reason till I Stop."

And pray to you, Apollo, first of indulgent fathers
to weep a thunderstruck son down from the high hots
on more horsepower than God could let run
and not fear. And also as the angel who backed
The Nine Sisters to all-time superstardom
on warehouses full of gold millionth albums
and a tax structure that could have saved England.

As you watched Daedalus once watch his boy down
from a high beyond warning, watched and remembered
    Phaeton
trailing a sky-scar, watched the man watch,
his eyes wind-watered but holding himself to flight-trim,
balancing slow cold turns down the hot shaft
the boy plunged, and hover at last too late
over the placeless water that had taken and closed . . . .

Grant us, father, not a denial of energy,
its space-trip spree above environment,
but a rest of purposes after the seized seizure,
the silence after the plunge without the plunge,
a fulfillment not necessarily final,
an excursion not from but to one another.
—I ask as a son in thy son's name for my son.

A Thanks to a Botanist

Setting his camera to blink a frame
every X minutes, his lights to a forcing pace,
he shot a reel of growth from seed to sere.
The Half Hour of the Zinnia. Up it rode,
slippering toward light, sliding from swelling pockets,
unfurling flowering hands from ends of thread,
holding them up to light, then letting fall,
and threads fall: a river system fled backward
to no system. Has God seen this
His distance from all fact? A man and camera
passed the miracle of the raised usual
and brought this near-weed to motion
and countermotion. As music is—
an ecology of emotion in balance.

Could a tree grow in thirty
held minutes of such blinking, that
would be a visible symphony.

86

Machine

It goes, all inside itself. It keeps touching
itself and stinks of it. The stink
moves a wheel that moves an arm that moves everything.

Or it hunches like a fetus and spins
its own umbilicus till it sparks.
Hands off, or it sizzles your hair straight!

Sometimes it turns its back, clicks,
and spits things down a chute.
It has many ways to its own kind.

Sometimes it breaks, battering itself
and must be stopped or we shall all
be saved. But it is always stopped. There is

no salvation. When it dies, we melt it
and make another that looks different
no better but does more of the same faster.

It can disguise itself as anything
but fools no one. There is always that look
of being inside itself, always that stink.

Bicentennial

This official bicentennial arts person programming
state-wide culturals for the up and coming
year-long Fourth of July, made an appointment,
and came, and I said I would (what I could),
and she said, "Are there any other New Jersey
poets we should mention?" And I said,
"Well, William Carlos Williams to start." And she:
"Has he published books?"
⠀⠀⠀⠀⠀⠀⠀⠀⠀⠀⠀⠀⠀⠀⠀⠀And I saw hall on hall
of stone glass buildings, a million offices
with labels on glass doors. And at the first desk
in every office, nothing. And beyond, in the inner
office, nothing. And a lost wind going, and doors

all swinging bang in the wind and swinging bang.
And at the end of every corridor
a wall of buttons blinking data dead.

Birthday

A fat sixty-year-old man woke me. "Hello,
Ugly," he said. I nodded. Ugly's easy.
"Why don't you punch yourself in the nose?" I said,
"You look like someone who would look better bloody."
"—And cantankerous," he said. "But just try it:
it's you will bleed." I shrugged. What difference
would that make? Everyone's bleeding something.

He saw me duck out the other side of the shrug.
"Where are you going?"—"Not far enough: I'll be back."
I climbed the maple that grew through our sidewalk once,
and looked at the river with Willy Crosby in it.
A man was diving. Two were in the boat:
one rowing, one working the hooks. The hooker shouted.
I was out of the tree and on the bank—where I'd been

before I remembered wrong. Willy was paler
than all the time I had taken to remember,
but I put on my Scout shirt and went to the wake.
It was better than the Senior Class Play later.
I got the part as the dead boy's best friend.
When his mother and father got tired of keening for Willy,
they turned and keened for me. "Oh, John," they wailed,

"your best friend's gone! Oh, Willy, poor John's here!
Come out and play!" I could have been with Willy,
as pale as he. And when he wouldn't come out,
they sang me to him. "Oh, Willy, we bought you a suit!
Oh, Willy, we bought you a bed with new silk sheets!
Oh, Willy, we bought you a house to put the bed in!
The house is too small! Come out and play with John!"

—"Why?" said the fat ugly sixty-year-old man.
"Not that I mind dramatics, but what's the point

of hamming it up without a line to tatter?"
"Goodbye," I said. He smirked. "Well, it's a start:
at least it's a speaking part. But it's not that easy.
I won't be said goodbye to. Not by you."
"No?" I said. "Just wait a little and see

how nothing it costs to kiss you off, friend. Meanwhile
—hello, Ugly." He nodded. "Ugly's easy.
Easier than climbing a tree that isn't there."
"It's there," I said. "Everything's always there."
"Your lines get better," he said, "but they stay pointless."
I shrugged: "You live by points . . . ." But he stopped me.
"Don't shrug away," he said, "There's nowhere to go."

Being Called
> A breakfast reverie in Key West

The Resident Dispenser of Bromides
being included in the general call
after yesterday's train wreck,
packed his bags and went running
with pink pills for the maimed.

What can I offer, doctors, but the will
to be included when the call comes?
Perhaps to assist at triage? At least
to pronounce the dead?—As the one-armed
surgeon still advises at transplants.

He could not bring himself to retire
after his accident. As God
stayed on after His to advise Tillich
on the good it does to do good
after it no longer matters

to Heaven or concept. It is not
not caring, but only that we are
futile. Like the movie queen
who lost her looks but kept old reels
for private viewing (it still runs on TV),

we try to remember as if we still were
what we remember. There is, of course,
power in a name. Once up in lights
it never dims entirely. The old
glow back in it. Late-Lates return it

to the young, who call it "funky," meaning
"hey, wow!" (but at root, "mildewed, earthy").
—Always that next jargon for saying again,
half-lively, what turns futile.
Would it be better not to say? not

to refuse the offered no-help
of good intention?—Not that I hurt,
or only a little, of some imagined
honesty. I am in Florida,
a February rose nodding

over my toast and coffee in a soft
expensive breeze I can afford,
in a sun I buy daily, gladly,
on a patio under a lime tree.
There is a pleasantness. With luck

it is a kindly long trip down
from cramming winter to this basking
knowledge of nothing. And from Miami
on the make-do transistor, a cracked
wrong quaver that began as Mozart.

October 18: Boston

. . . came gift-wrapped from the liquor store. A bum
who looked like Einstein in a trash can said,
"My need is great." I dropped change in his palm
—an acknowledgement of style—and he left it there.
"Like you," he said, "I need a jug. It's cold
under the bridge, and four bits is no heat."

It was argument in order. He had asked mercy.
I had given dismissal. I shifted my bottles,

90

dug out my wallet, found a five. "I'm Fritz,
in case we meet again," he said, "and we may
because I live again. Thank you in reason."

—I was paying for this performance. Why should he
have all the good lines? I'm an actor, too.
"In reason," I said, "die well."

                                    He had half-turned.
He half turned back. "Well," he said, "is soon.
As ill is dry. You're a philosopher,
or five bucks worth of something, and will yourself
learn in time enough."

                        —And left for the bridge.
Or wherever scene-stealers go to taste their triumph.

Scene Twelve: Take Seven

It is in its way like bumping into
an ex-wife in the lobby of the Ritz.
You do not go there often. For her
it is a habitat and she togged for it
by all of evolution. "Bill!" she says,
"how well you look!"—the grace
of all her small talk is also from evolution:
you know how you are looking, have settled for it.
What you cannot settle is what to remember
of how much you wanted, how little
you could at last bear.—Like that.
Exactly. Everything. All the way in the taxi
and train to the other mail slot, through which
you fall and lie unread, blaming no one,
knowing you were written with nothing to say.

Trying to Feel Something

Someone is always trying to feel something
or feeling something he'd rather not, and maybe
doesn't really—though how can one be sure?

Sylvia, John, and Anne did not entirely
invent what they felt.
          For a few hundred cash
the shrink my lawyer made me take my son to
as a first fiction toward getting him off probation
came up with "lacunae in the super-ego"
—meaning he lost his temper.
          So did I
listening to Judge Rocksoff, that illiterate
sac of mediocrity pomposing:
"This is Juvenile Court. I am Judge and Jury.
I say this evidence is incredulous. (sic)
—And you shut up!"
          But a thousand and some later
my son was a legal adult and was learning to hide
the pot he smoked. And a million ago Sylvia
inhaled her oven. And in another million,
Anne, her exhaust. And John went off the bridge-rail
at plus-or-minus some insolvency looking
for Hart Crane maybe. None of them entirely
invented their feeling, and two of them learned to write—
which can be relevant come time to appeal
the probations imposed upon us by the illiterate,
but does seem possibly a bit fanciful
to what I have just read, over morning coffee,
of a gent in a green Ford who last night,
having driven into the South Bronx by mistake
with the thermometer at almost ninety,
happened to hit and kill a dog, and then
forgot to keep going. He stopped to say he was sorry.

To prove which, some of the boys turned over the Ford
with him inside it, and having nothing to do,
set fire to it, and having nothing to do
and the weather too hot to do it, watched a while,

then watched the firemen come, and dumped some bricks—
not many and with no malice—from the roofs,
having nothing to do, and then it was all over
and only eleven o'clock or a bit after
and too hot for sleep, and what do you do next
but sit and invent the nothing there is to feel
about what wasn't really done in the first place?

—As I sit here in Metuchen and think to invent
something to feel about something I haven't entirely
made up from nothing—except, how does one know?
Isn't the news whatever we choose to notice?
I could have turned to the daily crossword puzzle
with nothing to feel but a generalized small sadness
for the failure of definition—which takes no feeling,
or we're enured to it, which comes to the same

except that my teachers told me and I in turn
told my students that if you want entirely
to learn to write (which can be something to do)
you must first feel something
                            except, what is there
this side of Anne's exhaust, Sylvia's oven,
John at the rail, Nixon in San Clemente,
Anne Frank and Cinderella at their chimneys,
and my coffee growing cold, which tastes blah,
though I drink it anyway for something to do?

Bashing the Babies
Easter, 1968

Sometimes you have hardly been born
when a king starts having dreams about you.
His troops get drunk then—they have to—
and a baby-crop sub-generation is torn
out of its mothers' screams and bashed:
orders are orders.
                    You yourself were rushed
out of the kingdom and lived to become a reader.

(I am a poet, and talk poetry. A man,
and talk chances. A son, and live as I can.
And was a soldier, killing for my leader.
And was taken by wrong parents, though their flight
is proof they could be sometimes, someways, right.)

I submit we should do or at least say
something deliberate and reasoned now
about the bashed babies. That it was they,
not we. That the feast is ours, you
its superintendent. I?—no one comes through
that infantry untouched. I am in this, too—
a father, a son, where every day
half-masted smokes wave masses, and the press
wires back body counts to the nearest guess.

It is Easter. I rise fat, rich,
hand out chocolate eggs, later drink coffee,
smoke. My dog gulps the poverty
of India heaped in an aluminum dish:
meat, egg, milk, cereal, bone meal,
cod liver oil.
                How shall we not feel
something for the babies who could not leave town?
who were not German Shepherds? who were hit
by their eggs and burned?
                        A few, of course, make out:
some mothers are shrewd hiders, some have known
a trooper—the occupied live as they can—
and even a drunken trooper is partly, in secret, a man.

But that evades the question. Being neither drunk
nor presently commanded, having run out
and made it to luck and, possibly, dispassion—what
do we do now? After creative funk?
After picketing flags? After burning the first draft
of everyone's card? After turning right? left?

We are—I believe you—one another's question.
How do we ask ourselves? Half-masted purple
burns from crosses. A genuflection
dips dark, rises golden. The spring-wound people
of Godthank heap flowers

in stone arches. "Come walk green,"
say the bashing bells of Sunday. "This world, ours
shines for you, questioner. What will you mean
by what you ask us? What shall we
mean by what we answer? What are we born to be?"

—I am a ghost, and talk vapors. An easy man
tossing a stick for a dog on an Easter lawn,
and talk my own babies, that they grew
chocolate-lucky. Your man, and talk you,
because we were together and got away
without being bashed, and would like to have something to say.

Any suggestions?—Well, have a good day.

A Magus

A missionary from the Mau Mau told me.
  There are spores blowing from space.
  He has himself seen an amazing botany
  springing the crust. Fruit with a bearded face
  that howls at the picker. Mushrooms that bleed.
  A tree of enormous roots that sends no trace
  above ground; not a leaf. And he showed me the seed
  of thorned lettuces that induce
  languages. The Jungle has come loose,
  is changing purpose.
                    Nor are the vegetations
  of the new continuum the only sign.
  New eyes have observed the constellations.
  And what does not change when looked at?—coastline?
  sea? sky? The propaganda of the wind reaches.
  Set watches on your gardens. What spring teaches
  seed shall make new verbs. A root is a tongue.

I repeat it as he spoke it. I do not interpret
  what I do not understand. He comes among
  many who have come to us. He speaks and we forget
  and are slow to be reminded. But he does come,
  signs do appear.

There are poisoned islands far over:
fish from their reefs come to table and some
glow in the dark not of candlelight. A windhover
chatters in the counters of our polar camps.
A lectern burns. Geese jam the radar. The red phone
rings. Is there an answer? Planes from black ramps
howl to the edge of sound. The unknown
air breaks from them. They crash through.
What time is it in orbit? Israeli teams
report they have found the body, but Easter seems
symbolically secure. Is a fact true?

How many megatons of idea is a man? What island
lies beyond his saying? I have heard, and say
what I heard said and believe. I do not understand.
But I have seen him change water to blood, and call away
the Lion from its Empire. He speaks that tongue.
I have seen white bird and black bird follow him, hung
like one cloud over his head. His hand,
when he wills it, bursts into flame. The white bird
and the black divide and circle it. At his word
they enter the fire and glow like metal. A ray
reaches from him to the top of the air,
and in it the figures of a vision play
these things I believe whose meaning I cannot say.

Then he closes his fist and there is nothing there.

The Week That Was

The pet shops were advertising non-rabid bats
for air-raid shelters. ("For that natural touch.")
LBJ and Mao were placing bets.
("The sky's the limit.") Overkill held her torch
high over the harbor. ("Give me your weak, your poor.")
England asked to be mentioned as a world power
and France said, *"Comment?"* (Transmitted as "No comment"
by the wire services, and botched by a lino-hack

to read "Con meant"—at which Parliament
took qualified umbrage until Nelson gets back.)

After that there was no more direct quotation.
It goes better in paraphrase. Evade the question:
you need no answer. And why speak
what's already in the junk mail?—Those bats sold.
And Norman Rockwell did a cover that week
of a boy and his pet hyena, both oddly soiled,
digging up an old sunset by a charred road.
Comment? No comment. This is pure mood.

January 1

If calendars are square holes, something
has slipped a round-peg late March morning
into this opening. A New Year's Day
smelling of wet root? I half look for crocuses,
glad not to find. We're wrong enough already.

By way of omen, we're one second late.
Astronomers ticked it onto the last minute
of the dead year. It's their accounting
for our eccentric rotation. As if one tick
could change us back to time. And yet in time—

in time enough—all seasons would drift loose
but for such finicals; as they did once
in Julian time, the vernal equinox
precessing through the centuries toward June.
We can learn to be more accurate than we have been.

Even corrected we're wrong. If that tick's true,
this day rings wrong to feeling. A New Year's Day
smelling of wet roots! Let the dog run it
as if gifts were free. I thumb a forsythia bud:
is it too soft for this side of sun shadow?

I mean to know. I get the pruning shears
and cut some stems to see if they will force.
Indoors again, I put them in a vase

and the vase on the mantel still decked out with holly,
the last dry scratch of Christmas. If this starts

let the dog shed—I may myself go bald
on gullied lawns—and leather apples shrivel
in the stubble of all season gone to random.
Just as it felt inside that astronomers' tick
added to the rung year, correcting zero.

The Sorrow of Obedience

The lieutenant ordered me to ask Abdhul
    if he would sell one of the speckled puppies
    his mongrel bitch was mothering.

As I waited for Abdhul to finish cleaning his rifle
    —he is known to be testy—I reviewed the difference
    between "puppy/son of a dog" and "bitch/mother."

Obedience, as even generals must understand,
    is no substitute for idiom. I translated,
    praying to get it right once. When, however,

Abdhul first shot the lieutenant, then slit his throat,
    then lopped his sex and threw the mess to the mongrel,
    I was once more left to grieve for my imperfections.

On Passion As a Literary Tradition

Asked by a reporter out of questions
to name the one thing most important to art,
Lytton Strachey, an old man with the voice
of an uncracked boy soprano, trebled, "Passion!"

It *can* treble. There's no one place on the scale
where burning starts. It can sound silly
and still be what it is. But what is it?
Housman said he had to be careful while shaving

not to think of poetry. A line
could shake him till he nicked himself.
If it cuts, it must be something. Not-much
can be enough to bleed for.

                    Foghorn Odysseus
(he *had* to be gravel throated) nocking arrows
like check marks down the guest list, did what he did
and said nothing about it. He growled instructions
to have the mess cleaned up, and took a bath.

Nikos Kazantzakis, in his version,
had a lot to say about his hair, like fire
up from the crotch to a black smoke in the armpits.
But Odysseus only grunted and reached for a towel.

Whatever passion is, it needn't tremble.
It slashes more than it nicks, can tear the guts
out of the nothing said. If you could say it,
it wouldn't be what you meant. It's a fire

that curls like hair on ape-man. It's mostly tiresome.
You need it like adrenalin when you need it
for getting up the tree ahead of the bear
who sniffs and decides you wouldn't be worth the climb.

—Or so you hope. Once then the beast is gone,
the sooner you stop pumping the stuff, the better
you'll find your bearings out of the fangy woods,
and go home to nick yourself on poetry.

BANG BANG

Elegy Just in Case

Here lie Ciardi's pearly bones
In their ripe organic mess.
Jungle blown, his chromosomes
Breed to a new address.

Was it bullets or a wind
Or a rip cord fouled on chance?
Artifacts the natives find
Decorate them when they dance.

Here lies the sgt.'s mortal wreck
Lily spiked and termite kissed,
Spiders pendant from his neck
And a beetle on his wrist.

Bring the tick and southern flies
Where the land crabs run unmourning
Through a night of jungle skies
To a climeless morning.

And bring the chalked eraser here
Fresh from rubbing out his name.
Burn the crew-board for a bier.
(Also Colonel what's-his-name.)

Let no dice be stored and still.
Let no poker deck be torn.
But pour the smuggled rye until
The barracks threshold is outworn.

File the papers, pack the clothes,
Send the coded word through air—
"We regret and no one knows
Where the sgt. goes from here."

"Missing as of inst. oblige,
Deepest sorrow and remain—"
Shall I grin at persiflage?
Could I have my skin again

Would I choose a business form
Stilted mute as a giraffe,

Or a pinstripe unicorn
On a cashier's epitaph?

Darling, darling, just in case
Rivets fail or engines burn,
I forget the time and place
But your flesh was sweet to learn.

Swift and single as a shark
I have seen you churn my sleep
Now if beetles hunt my dark
What will beetles find to keep?

Fractured meat and open bone—
Nothing single or surprised.
Fragments of a written stone
Undeciphered but surmised.

Sea Burial

Through the sea's crust of prisms looking up
Into the run of light above the swell
And down a fathom, down a fathom more
Until the darkness closes like a shell.

Oblique, like fall of leaves down the wet glide
Of season and surrender from the tree
Of life across the windows of a wind
To the final ruined lawn beneath a sea.

Glide, glide and fall. How lightly death goes down
Into the crushing fog, pale and refracted.
Seen dimly and then lost, like jellyfish
Flowering a tide, expanded, then contracted,

Once more expanded, and then closed forever
To make a stain on stone and liquefy
The memory that kissed a mountain girl
And ran on grass as if it could not die.

Measurements

I've zeroed an altimeter on the floor
then raised it to a table and read *three feet.*
Nothing but music knows what air is
more precisely than this. I read on its face
Sensitive Altimeter and believe it.

Once on a clear day over Arkansas
I watched the ridges on the radar screen,
then looked down from the blister and hung like prayer:
the instrument was perfect: ridge by ridge
the electric land was true as the land it took from.

These, I am persuaded, are instances
round as the eye to see with,
perfections of one place in the visited world
and omens to the godly
teaching an increase of possibility.

I imagine that when a civilization
equal to its instruments is born
we may prepare to build such cities as music
arrives to on the air, lands where we are
the instruments of April in the seed.

V–J Day

On the tallest day in time the dead came back.
Clouds met us in the pastures past a world.
By short wave the releases of a rack
Exploded on the interphone's new word.

Halfway past Iwo we jettisoned to sea
Our gift of bombs like tears and tears like bombs
To spring a frolic fountain daintily
Out of the blue metallic seas of doom.

No fire-shot cloud pursued us going home.
No cities cringed and wallowed in the flame.

Far out to sea a blank millennium
Changed us alive, and left us still the same.

Lightened, we banked like jays, antennae squawking.
The four wild metal halos of our props
Blurred into time. The interphone was talking
Abracadabra to the cumulus tops:

Dreamboat three-one to Yearsend—loud and clear,
Angels one-two, on course at one-six-nine.
Magellan to Balboa. Propwash to Century.
How do you read me? Bombay to Valentine.

Fading and out. And all the dead were homing.
(*Wisecrack to Halfmast. Doom to Memory.*)
On the tallest day in time we saw them coming,
Wheels jammed and flaming on a metal sea.

Citation on Retirement

Light-Colonel Trinkett, you there
in the toe-crud of God's clay
feet, you ooze sliming the cellar
of data's orphan asylum, you loose
button of bloody threads numbering
haircuts to a follicle, you parade-rest
battalion of Wassermann positives
at close order bedcheck zeroing in
demerit by demerit on a
recoilless maximum-velocity
fart in ranks; you light-stain,
belted-jelly leaking, ameoba,
virus, phagocyte, amino, ferment, down
porcelain filters to
chemistry's last edge of almost
life
        what's after you is back
to building blocks, space dust
in the galaxy of an alga's stoma
in the universe of a shrimp's rectum.

106

Cross over, I say. Not drop dead—
that takes fallible substance—but
drain down one more
hole wrapped in a hole back to
exactly identified nothing

for the good of the service.

On a Photo of Sgt. Ciardi a Year Later

The sgt. stands so fluently in leather,
So poster-holstered and so newsreel-jawed
As death's costumed and fashionable brother,
My civil memory is overawed.

Behind him see the circuses of doom
Dance a finale chorus on the sun.
He leans on gun sights, doesn't give a damn
For dice or stripes, and waits to see the fun.

The cameraman whose ornate public eye
Invented that fine bravura look of calm
At murderous clocks hung ticking in the sky
Palmed the deception off without a qualm.

Even the camera, focused and exact
To a two dimensional conclusion,
Uttered its formula of physical fact
Only to lend data to illusion.

The camera always lies. By a law of perception
The obvious surface is always an optical ruse.
The leather was living tissue in its own dimension,
The holsters held benzedrine tablets, the guns were no use.

The careful slouch and dangling cigarette
Were always superstitious as Amen.
The shadow under the shadow is never caught:
The camera photographs the cameraman.

A Box Comes Home

I remember the United States of America
As a flag-draped box with Arthur in it
And six marines to bear it on their shoulders.

I wonder how someone once came to remember
The Empire of the East and the Empire of the West.
As an urn maybe delivered by chariot.

You could bring Germany back on a shield once
And France in a plume. England, I suppose,
Kept coming back a long time as a letter.

Once I saw Arthur dressed as the United States
Of America. Now I see the United States
Of America as Arthur in a flag-sealed domino.

And I would pray more good of Arthur
Than I can wholly believe. I would pray
An agreement with the United States of America

To equal Arthur's living as it equals his dying
At the red-taped grave in Woodmere
By the rain and oakleaves on the domino.

An Island Galaxy

Once on Saipan at the end of the rains
I came on a flooded tire rut in a field
and found it boiling with a galaxy
of pollywogs, each millionth micro-dot
avid and home in an original swarm.

For twenty yards between the sodden tents
and a coral cliff, a universe ran on
in a forgotten dent of someone's passing.
Clusters and nebulae of whirligigs
whorled and maddened, a burst gas of life

from the night hop of unholdable energy.
Did one frog squatting heavy at the full

of its dark let out this light, these black rapids
inside the heart of light in the light-struck dent
of the accidental and awakened waters?

There on the island of our burning, in man's place
in the fire-swarm of war, and in a sunburst
lens, I stood asking—what? Nothing.
Universes happen. Happen and are come upon.
I stood in the happening of no imagination.

Ten days later, having crossed two seas,
I passed that rut again. The sun had burned
the waters back to order. The rut lay baked.
Twenty upthrust shoreline yards of time
slept in the noon of a misplaced intention.

And the bed and the raised faces of the world
lay stippled with the dry seals of the dead,
black wafers with black ribbons, as if affixed
to a last writ, but with such waste of law,
I could not read its reasons for its proofs.

A Memory of the Sad Chair

All in a dream of the time it was
(Kissing the corpse on its bombproof nose)
I winked at a peach that gave me a buzz,
But when I rubbed her she had no fuzz.
A sad chair stared, heaped with our clothes.

All in the light of the moon that came
(The bottles empty, the switches thrown)
I lost my wallet, I changed my name,
I saw the colonel go down aflame.
There stood the chair, our only one.

All in a heap on the chair that stood
(Polaris neither rising nor setting)
I told no evil, I saw no good
Except those sad few sticks of wood,
Like a ghost I had been forgetting.

All in a row in the law that wrought
(Some still listed and some still lost)
I sighted squinty, my tracers caught,
The sad chair blew up like a thought.
She snored her whiskey. I turned and tossed.

All in a dream of the thought that blows
The moon in the window, the ghost on the chair,
The one sad chair heaped with our clothes,
I kissed her corpse on its bombproof nose,
And left her dead and went out for air.

All in a dream of the time it is
(The colonels coming, the colonels going)
Since Tokyo sizzled her star-spangled sizz,
I got a medal for writing this,
And an oak-leaf cluster because it was snowing.

All in the hush of the snow that fell
(Tojo dancing for everyone's crime)
We swung the hammer, we rang the bell,
But the only reason it wasn't Hell
We went to was—we won, that time.

All in a haggle of what we won
(The corncob rampant above the noose)
The sad chair stood, our only one
I wish, now all is said and done,
We had shared that sadness, but what's the use?

To Lucasta, About That War

A long winter from home the gulls blew
    on their brinks, the tankers slid
    over the hump where the wolf packs hid
    like voodoo talking, the surf threw
    bundles with eyes ashore. I did
what booze brought me, and it wasn't you.

I was mostly bored. I watched and told time
    as enforced, a swag-man

110

under the clock. The bloat-bags ran
wet from nowhere, selling three-for-a-dime
and nobody buying. Armies can
type faster than men die, I'm

told, and can prove. Didn't I find
time there, and more, to count
all, triplicate, and still walk guard-mount
on the gull- and drum-wind
over the hump? I did, and won't
deny several (or more) pig-blind

alleys with doors, faces, dickers,
which during, the ships slid
over the hump where the packs hid.
And talking voodoo and snickers
over the edge of their welts, I did
what I could with (they called them) knickers;

and it was no goddamn good,
and not bad either. It
was war (they called it) and it lit
a sort of skyline somehow in the blood,
and I typed the dead out a bit
faster than they came—just keeping ahead—

and the gulls blew high on their brinks,
and the ships slid, and the surf threw,
and the Army initialed, and you
were variously, vicariously, and straight and with kinks,
raped, fondled, and apologized to—
which is called (as noted) war. And it stinks.

Childe Horvald to the Dark Tower Came

Well, they loaded him with armor and left him
All night by the altar rail, and he was young,
And darks have voices when you pray to hear them,
And in the morning his lord unbuckled

And blessed his shoulder, and most were drunk yet
From the night wassail, and all the girls . . . .

At, say, sixteen can you doubt the dark and the girls?
The grail, they told him, *the grail.* And he: *I swear it.*

And so the tower rose beyond his dead horse
In the valley of drifted bones. He blew his horn then
(Noise of the true man), and unbuckled, and came twirling
The folderol sword hilted with girls' garlands
And of course *Blut und Ehre* sloganed on it,
And worse nonsense brave in his head.
                                                    And what would you
Do if you were the magician hearing
His boy-murderous blast shaking your phials and silences,
Watching him come shouting *St. Poobah and the dragon!*
Into your library and uncertainty?
                                        It takes
More than civility to civilize
The very young. I say send out a peri
If you've her address or her incantation,
Or drug him if you can, or conjure him on
To the bog of his own idiocy. But for Godsake
Don't let him into the house with his nice profile
All tensed for swordplay and lifting of heads
At arm's length over the fallen books.

Or if you've real
Magic, change him! change him!

Naples

> *Hanno vinto le mosche*

I saw at a table of the bombed café
a fat man in shirtsleeves,
the stuff of his jersey sweated
to his woman's breasts and belly
so close that the texture of the fat
(like the texture of cottage cheese

or of brains or of boiled cauliflower)
showed through the cloth.

All he had chewed and swallowed
lay ruined in the fat
which pressed at his skin for escape,
a skin strung on a net
of round holes, while through the holes
the fat pressed for escape
held only by the strands of the net
through which, perhaps, his blood ran.

The air was soaked heavy
with the oil-sweet smell of corpses,
that taint which breathes from all
the summer cities of ruin,
their rubble and broken sewerage.
He sat at a table of the bombed café
brushing away the flies that came for him.
Especially for him. There were no others.

He wore his cloud of flies
as a saint wears patience
after his knees have been abused
too long to feel the pain itself.
The flies were his vocation
and he theirs. There can be no
accident in so much meeting:
he was a St. Anthony of flies.

And all of ruined Europe fell about him.
Tiles lay wedged in the gross ruff
at the back of his neck. The dust
of an exploded temple caked
muddy on his bald head and flowed
like half-thickened blood
down and over his eyes,
which were sealed in his fat like navels.

He sat at a table of the bombed café
by the ruined temple, a pediment at his feet,
its writing cracked and crazed. His chair
was a split capital. When he waved his arm

to brush away the flies
a column fell. When he waved it back
another. From every crash the dust
changed into flies and drew a cloud about him.

Survival in Missouri

When Willie Crosby died I thought too much:
Sister and Mother and Uncle and Father O'Brien
All talked about me and how
It was all very touching: *Such sorrow.*
He really lived in that boy.
Here now, you gowonoff to the movies.
Give your grief to God.

But here I am in Missouri twenty years later
Watching the rain come down
That no one prayed for: a drowned crop
And the Mississippi rising
On a wet world still washing away the kid
Who thought too much about Willie Crosby
But went to the movies all the same.
It was a lovely wake and everyone admired me.

At dusk the Salt Hills thin blue and far.
Having survived a theology and a war,
I am beginning to understand
The rain.

The Baboon and the State

A dog snout puzzles out the look of a man.
The wrong smell of a stranger tweaks the air.
"Fangs! Fangs! Why should we run? We are
Born of the chosen, first, and tallest tree!
Sons of the Sacred Banyan follow me!
Baboons are born to kill because they can."

114

Clemenceau said to the American
With the blue jaw and the fox-terrier hair,
"Above France, civilization." He made war
As if he strangled a mistress—tenderly,
But with a certain competence. A man
Must sacrifice for his own family.

Guido came trembling from the Vatican,
Roped up for God, God's moonspot in his hair.
"How shall I overthrow the Lateran?"
The Fat Pope said. "Speak up. God lives in me.
In His name teach me my cupidity."
And Guido spilled the malice in his ear.

Odysseus, that seven-minded man,
Piled up his kills to honor prophecy—
An indispensable, most Ithacan
Justification for a blood at war.
He spoke tongues and heard God-talk on the air,
But all his men were told was, "Follow me!"

Is man wrong for the State, or it for man?
High reasons and low causes make a war.
It is the Baboon kills, because he can
But Presidents hear voices from the air.
So packs and parishes cry equally:
"God's first and last Law sounded from Our Tree."

The voices come to rest where they began.
Clemenceau nods to the American.
Guido comes praying from the Vatican.
An indispensable most Ithacan
Baboon snout puzzles out the look of a man.
The killers kill. They kill because they can.

The Gift

In 1945, when the keepers cried *kaput*,
Josef Stein, poet, came out of Dachau
like half a resurrection, his other
eighty pounds still in their invisible grave.

Slowly then the mouth opened and first
a broth, and then a medication, and then
a diet, and all in time and the knitting mercies,
the showing bones were buried back in flesh,

and the miracle was finished. Josef Stein,
man and poet, rose, walked, and could even
beget, and did, and died later of other causes
only partly traceable to his first death.

He noted—with some surprise at first—
that strangers could not tell he had died once.
He returned to his post in the library, drank his beer,
published three poems in a French magazine,

and was very kind to the son who at last was his.
In the spent of one night he wrote three propositions:
That Hell is the denial of the ordinary. That nothing lasts.
That clean white paper waiting under a pen

is the gift beyond history and hurt and heaven.

CONVERSATIONS

Memo: Preliminary Draft of a Prayer to God the Father

Sir, it is raining tonight in Towson, Maryland.
It rained all the way from Atlanta, the road steaming
slicks and blindnesses, almost enough to slow for.
Thank you for the expensive car, its weight and sure tread
that make it reasonable to go reasonably fast.

My wife is in Missouri. She flew there yesterday
because her parents are eighty, terminal,
and no longer sure of what they were always sure of.
Thank you for airline tickets, rental cars,
the basic credit cards, a checking balance.

We doubt they can live much longer and not well.
I, too, have learned to love them. Thank you
for the wet roads to mercy on which I buy
the daughter home to the last of mother and father.
I wish I had such destinations left me.

I phoned my son at home tonight, the younger.
He has been busted for pot again. His fourth time.
There is, however, a lawyer, a reliable fixer.
He will cost me only another three days on this road.
Thank you for the road, the bad lunches, and the pleasant
        ladies.

I phoned my older son in Boston. He has wrecked his car
and has not learned to walk. His apartment, you see,
is almost a mile from school. He will miss classes.
Thank you for the classes he will not miss
if I ask my agent to book me a tour in April.

I phoned my daughter in New York. She is happy
but needs more voice lessons, and a piano.
She could make do with her guitar, but less well.
Thank you for everything she is dreaming of dreaming
and for the unanswered letter from California.

I will answer yes when I get home. The lessons
will come from pocket money. The piano
is waiting there in Claremont in February.

Thank you for Claremont and choices and for this daughter
and for the road I go well enough as things go.

I mean, sir, it does lead on, and I thank you.
It is not what I imagined. It may be better.
Better, certainly, than what I remember from starting.
At times, I confess, it is slightly depressing. The ladies
who are only slightly brittle and slightly silly,

but on any reasonable scale bright and admirable,
depress me slightly. But so do my own bad habits
when I am left to them freely. I do not complain:
I describe. I am grateful but imperfect and, therefore,
imperfectly grateful. It is all good enough

and I thank you, sir. If you are ever in Towson,
I can recommend the high level mediocrity
of the Quality Inn Motel just off the Beltway.
It is only slightly embalmed. It is clean and quiet.
With the TV on you do not hear the rain.

A Conversation with Leonardo

It was a stew of a night. The power failed,
killing the air conditioner. And the windows sealed.
I flailed off the one sheet and lay spread-eagled.

The instant I wilted to sleep Leonardo pounced,
drew his circle round me on the sheet,
tried fitting hands, feet, head to one turned ratio.

Ah, the greatness of lost causes! "I could have told you,"
I said, "if what you're after is ideal proportion,
you're sketching the wrong times." He frowned.

"A collector," he said, "can always use deformity
among examples, but only if lost within it
there hides a memory of man to illustrate."

"You are thinking," I said, "of Praxiteles, and beyond,
to that business of God's image, which is harmony
as measured by the famous scholastic hole

120

in Plato's head, where nothing is really real
but the abstraction of nothing—of the idea
of the abstraction of nothing—to an absolute.

After you, blessed maestro, came genre—the thing
measured not by absolutes but by other examples
of the same school. I am, alas, *that* man."

"Forgive me," he said, "I seem to hear you claim
an absolute irrelevance as a poor excuse
for what there's no excuse for." "None," I said,

"but a reverence for what was never there.
God measures perfection and crock measures pot."
—"You make me grateful I died in God's formed day."

"Master," I answered, "do you imagine God
is thinking you in this sequence? I'm
thinking you, more reverently, I daresay,

than He would be inclined to, were He inclined."
He looked away. "If I sense what you mean,
I am obliged to add that the thought disturbs me."

"Great Soul," I said, "how else could we have fallen
out of your circle but in that same disturbance
no man asked for and none yet has welcomed?"

"Thank you for a theme," he said. "I shall try
a drawing of it. If it lives on paper—
if I can make it live—I may understand."

"I wish I could hold to this same dream," I told him,
"Until it contains that drawing." "Perhaps," he said,
"it will be in one that comes later." "I will live for that,"

I said. But woke. The air was soup. The power still off.
It was pointless to try for sleep again in nature.
I went down and opened a bottle and sat to the dark.

Talking Myself to Sleep at One More Hilton

I have a country but no town.
Home ran away from me. My trees
ripped up their white roots and lay down.
Bulldozers cut my lawn. All these
are data toward some sentiment
like money: God knows where it went.

There was a house as sure as time.
Sure as my father's name and grave.
Sure as trees for me to climb.
Sure as behave and misbehave.
Sure as lamb stew. Sure as sin.
As warts. As games. As a scraped shin.

There was a house, a chicken run,
a garden, guilt, a rocking chair.
I had six dogs and every one
was killed in traffic. I knew where
their bones were once. Now I'm not sure.
Roses used them for manure.

There was a house early and late.
One day there came an overpass.
It snatched the stew right off my plate.
It snatched the plate. A whiff of gas
blew up the house like a freak wind.
I wonder if I really mind.

My father died. My father's house
fell out of any real estate.
My dogs lie buried where time was
when time still flowed, where now a slate
stiff river loops, called Exit Nine.
Why should I mind? It isn't mine.

I have the way I think I live.
The doors of my expense account
open like arms when I arrive.
There is no cloud I cannot mount
and sip good bourbon as I ride.
My father's house is Hilton-wide.

What are old dog bones? Were my trees
still standing would I really care?
What's the right name for this disease
of wishing they might still be there
if I went back, though I will not
and never meant to?—Smash the pot,

knock in the windows, blow the doors.
I am not and mean not to be
what I was once. I have two shores
five hours apart, soon to be three.
And home is anywhere between.
Sure as the airport limousine,

sure as credit, sure as a drink,
as the best steak you ever had,
as thinking—when there's time to think—
it's good enough. At least not bad.
Better than dog bones and lamb stew.
It does. Or it will have to do.

Back through the Looking Glass to This Side

Yesterday, in a big market, I made seven thousand dollars
while I was flying to Dallas to speak to some lunch group
and back for a nightcap with my wife. A man from Dallas
sat by me both ways, the first from Campbell's Soup,
the other from some labeled can of his own, mostly water,
and Goldwater at that. Capt. J.J. Slaughter

of Untied Airlines kept us all in smooth air and well
and insistently informed of our progress. Miss G. Klaus
brought us bourbon on ice, and snacks. At the hotel
the lunch grouped and the group lunched. I was,
if I may say so, perceptive, eloquent, sincere.
Then back to the airport with seventeen minutes to spare.

Capt. T.V. Ringo took over with Miss P. Simbus
and that Goldwater oaf. We made it to Newark at nine

plus a few minutes lost in skirting cumulonimbus
in our descent at the Maryland-Delaware line.
"Ticker runs late," said the horoscope page. "New highs
posted on a broad front."—So the good guys

had won again! Fat, complacent, a check
for more than my father's estate in my inside pocket,
with the launched group's thanks for a good day's work,
I found my car in the lot and poked it
into the lunatic aisles of U.S. 1,
a good guy coming home, the long day done.

Dialogue with Outer Space

Do you?
    Yes.
        Do you what?
            Whatever—
to the unqualified question the unqualified answer.
I do.
    Everything?
        Yes.
        Every*thing?*
            I do.
In the fact or the thought of it—everything.
What is done in fact without thought, in place of
thought. What is done thoughtfully, premeditatively
in fact. Or in thought only, to escape fact,
to make it bearable, to seduce it—everything.
And do you now confess?
        To myself, everything.
To the world in practical fact what is in its own terms
convenient. Except that in an anger like an assault
of honesty I do now and then not care and do openly
admit being and having been and meaning to be everything,
and to relive it.
    You have lied?
        I recall that life.

Cheated?
     And that one.
          Stolen?
              Negligently.
What has there been that would have been worth the time
it would have taken to steal it?
              But you have?
Sometimes there was something?
              At times. A trifle.
And always instantly not worth keeping.
You have killed?
          Always alas for the wrong reasons.
For what reasons?
          For duty. For my captain's approval.
Not for survival?
          Survival lay with my captain,
the controls his. I killed because I could.
You were proud?
          For no reason I have not survived.
Envious?
     At times, but I have admired many.
Wrathful?
      In bursts from the sperm center. A screeing
of sensation like Morse Code drowned in a cosmic whine.
Slothful?
     Yawningly when that was my mood's pleasure.
Avaricious?
     No.
          Gluttonous?
            Hungry.
              Lustful?
                Gladly.
What then do you believe should be done with your soul?
Erase its name and make way for another experience.
Why?
     First, because it is completed and time is not.
And second?
      Because it will in any case be erased.
And third?
      Because, though it does not matter, eternity
would be the one experience beyond mercy.

And you beg mercy?

      I do.

          Why?

               Because I was born.

Driving across the American Desert and Thinking of the Sahara

I hang the cloth water bag from the door mirror.
A seepage evaporates. By wasting a little,
and having a wind to my going, I cool—
almost to freshness—what I live by.

I cross bone dusts to rimrock,
leaving a storm of dust in my rear vision.
I breathe some million molecules of argon
breathed by Christ once. Part of His pronunciation.

The dust of saints' brain cells is also a matter of fact.
I rinse it from my throat, let the water bag swing to the wind,
its strap tilting the mirror to sky. I adjust it
back to the storm I make and forever leave.

At sundown in an oasis of green money
girls silvery as frost on pewter goblets
smile me from passage to a made air,
time and space filtered from it.

I pay gladly for absolution
from saints' grit, rimrock, the sucking sun
burning the storm I stirred and outran
the other side of this filter we change through

from what lies open, where any man
can feel his immortalities sucked like water
to gather and fall again—and who knows where?—
till even the sun we can bear some of

126

gasps; and it, unchangeable argon, bone dust,
saint dust, dust of the last idea,
drift wide gravities that will—somewhere
outside dens we come to—form again.

Washing Your Feet

Washing your feet is hard when you get fat.
                    *   *   *
In lither times the act was unstrained and pleasurable.
                    *   *   *
You spread the toes for signs of athlete's foot.
                    *   *   *
You used creams, and rubbing alcohol, and you powdered.
                    *   *   *
You bent over, all in order, and did everything.
                    *   *   *
Mary Magdalene made a prayer meeting of it.
                    *   *   *
She, of course, was washing not her feet but God's.
                    *   *   *
Degas painted ladies washing their own feet.
                    *   *   *
Somehow they also seem to be washing God's feet.
                    *   *   *
To touch any body anywhere should be ritual.
                    *   *   *
To touch one's own body anywhere should be ritual.
                    *   *   *
Fat makes the ritual wheezy and a bit ridiculous.
                    *   *   *
Ritual and its idea should breathe easy.
                    *   *   *
They are memorial, meditative, immortal.
                    *   *   *
Toenails keep growing after one is dead.
                    *   *   *
Washing my feet, I think of immortal toenails.
                    *   *   *
What are they doing on these ten crimped polyps?
                    *   *   *
I reach to wash them and begin to wheeze.
                    *   *   *

I wish I could paint like Degas or believe like Mary.
$$* \quad * \quad *$$
It is sad to be naked and to lack talent.
$$* \quad * \quad *$$
It is sad to be fat and to have dirty feet.

Tenzone

Soul to Body

That affable, vital, inspired even, and well-paid
    persuader of sensibility with the witty asides
but, at core, lucent and unswayed—
    a gem of serenest ray—besides
    being the well-known poet, critic, editor, and middle-high
    aesthete of the circuit is, alas, I.

Some weep for him: a waster of talent. Some
    snicker at the thought of talent in him. He leaves
in a Cadillac, has his home away from home
    where the dolls are, and likes it. What weaves
    vine leaves in the hair weaves no laurel for the head.
    The greedy pig, he might as well be dead—

to art at least—for wanting it all and more—
    cash, bourbon, his whim away from whom.
He's a belly, a wallet, a suit, a no-score
    of the soul. Sure, he looks like a boom
    coming, but whatever he comes to, sits to, tries
    to sit still to and say, is a bust. It's booby prize

time at the last dance whenever he
    lets a silence into himself. It grinds
against the jitter in him and dies. Poetry
    is what he gabs at, then dabbles in when he finds
    hobby time for it between serious pitches
    for cash, free-loading, and the more expensive bitches.

I give him up, say I. (And so say I.)
    There are no tears in him. If he does feel,
he's busier at Chateaubriand than at asking why.
    He lives the way he lives as if it were real.

A con man. A half-truth. A swindler in the clear.
Look at him guzzle. He actually likes it here!

BODY TO SOUL

That grave, secretive, aspirant even, and bang-kneed
    eternalist of boneyards with the swallowed tongue
but, at dream source, flaming and fire-freed—
    a monk of dark-celled rays—along
    with being heretic, ignorant, Jesuit, and who-
knows-what skeleton, is, alas, not wholly you.

I've watched you: a scratcher of scabs that are not
    there. An ectoplasmic jitter. Who was it spent
those twenty years and more in the polyglot
    of nightmares talking to Pa? If I went
    over your head to God, it *was* over your head.
Whose butt grew stiff in the chair the nights you read

whose eyes blind and wrote whose nerves to a dither?
    And who got up in the cold to revise you by light?
You're a glowworm. A spook. A half-strung zither
    with a warped sounding box: you pluck all right
    but if what whines out is music, an alley cat
in moon-heat on a trashcan is Kirsten Flagstadt.

Yes, I like it here. Make it twenty times worse
    and I'd still do it over again, even with you
like a monkey on my back. You dried-out wet-nurse,
    think you're the poet, do you? You're wind that blew
    on ashes that wouldn't catch. You were gone
the instant I learned the poem is belly and bone.

I gave *you* up. Like a burp. For a better weather
    inside my guts. And, yes, I want it all—
grab, gaggle, and rut—as sure as death's no breather.
    Though you wouldn't know, being dead as yesterday's
        squall
    where the sea's a diamond-spilling toss in the bright brace
of today's air, to glitter me time and place.

Minus One

Of seven sparrows on a country wire
    and off in the instant ruffle
of hawk shadow, one was no flyer,
    or not enough, or was lost in the shuffle,
six stunted their little panics one spin
    around a pasture and an oak, and spun
back to whatever they had been
    in much the same row minus one.

        Is there a kismet
    the size of one of seven
        sparrows? Is it
    written before heaven,
        swami, in the mystic
            billion ungiven
    Names? Is there a loving statistic
        we are motes of?
    Whatever remembers us, finally, is enough.
    If anything remembers, something is love.

Meanwhile a shadow comes to a point,
    to beak and talons. Seven surprises
start and one stops. Six joint
    excursions circle a crisis
they return forgetting. And what am I
    remembering? It was not on me
the shadow dove. I can sit by
    noting statistically.

        Is there an average
    the size of one? of any?
        Is there no rage
    against numbers? Of many
    motes, mathematician,
        shall none be
more than decided? for once its own decision?
        I have spun loose
again and again with your sparrows, father, and whose
hawk is this now? unchosen? come to choose?

Blue Movie

There is no cause for love in such a script,
nor even for much transition. Two girls come
mincing in crinoline to a pool. Stripped
as if on truant impulse, frolicsome
(the camera zooming in on clefts and hair),
they wet a toe and show the water's cold
by hugging one another in play, till bare
touch to bare touch tingles, and they fold

together on the moss bank and lie panting.
Their white hams, like their hamming, twitch and tremble
till teasing teases something like true wanting.
Not all of even this flesh can dissemble.
Some part of false touch touches. Thighs outflung
to camera angles, they squirm public meat
till they are tongue to crotch and crotch to tongue,
their bellies beaded wet in a made heat.

Cut to two lordly hunters in the wings,
a camera on their flies, which they unzip
with that same cueing from the first of things
that says, "No introductions, boys. Just strip."
And *ooh* and *aah*, the maidens (only started
by girlish mere contrivance) flit away
behind a bush. (No, they have not departed:
they run to show the cameras what will stay.)

The hunters and their finger-beckoned bunnies
wet one another. For such juices once
the gods came down. Now, retold in the funnies,
Leda and Europa, two coy cunts,
having been spread and had, work up to tricks.
Drooling at the boys' crotches all a-wiggle,
they beg the unwilted gods, and those rock pricks
pump their assholes while the humped girls giggle.

There, while mythologies teach them their Greek,
they French kiss like two chums at boarding school.
The camera, in a high artistic streak
flashes a hot montage of ass, tit, tool,

the kissing girls, and their ooh-la-la eyes.
Enter, of course, two other hunters then—
it's the quail season. Still quick to surprise,
the girls, still bashful, hug and cry, "Ooh—men!"

The rest is variations of no art
at easy orifices, one by one,
and two by two. A shock of flesh to start,
then bald redundancy. In tireless fun
the flesh assembles, joins, and then untangles
to start again, stretched skins of pure intent.
Their one lie is that nothing ever dangles
but outyearns Keats, in spending still unspent.

Till the director, bored to the point of wit,
works up a last touch. When the hunters go,
still cocky after twelve dives in the pit,
he shows the broads arranged in a tableau
of innocence undone by bestial rape.
Strewn like husks and separate on their bed
of swallowing moss, they sink to dark and gape
the disassembled gestures of the dead.

An Apology for Not Invoking the Muse

Erato popped in. What a talent for suspicion!
"Now what?" she said. I thought I knew.
"I am writing an unimportant poem," I told her.

She slammed her lute down on my desk.
Slammed it so hard it shook the air forever.
Even in anger she gives off such sounds.

I cannot summon an adequate emotion
except in sensing how all loss belittles
what's left to make a truth of.

"Who authorized that?" she wanted to know.
"Honey," I said, "do I have to check with you
before I scratch an itch? This was a small one

"in a minor crease I needn't specify
except to say we all have some—I mean
we mortals—and they do burn."

Was I being unreasonable? She chose to wail.
"Four thousand years of lute lessons in those crags
in a suffered dream of tuning types like you,

"and you show your gratitude by scratching creases!"
—Nothing is more demanding than a woman
who has given everything. Yet, how she glowed!

"Darling," I said, "you were born to natural grandeur.
I worship you for it. Gratefully. I've prayed
to be worthy of you. It's no use:

"I am small, dull, subject to gravity, and locked
in these creases that itch and must be scratched
by those who haven't had your advantages.

"Besides—may I add?—this unimportant poem
is outbulging Doric proportion. Less
would be better than more, being more to the fact."

She glared nobility. "Are you one of mine,
and still dare speak of unimportant poems?
The least song, clod, consumes the singer!"

"Angel," I pleaded, "not everything's an *Aeneid*—
which would make it Calliope's business, to begin with . . . ."
She flatted: "You leave my sister out of this!"

"I mean, I love you most for the sweet small
that trembles to a silence it awakens
and echoes back a ghost, when you let me say it."

"*I* let you say it! You didn't even invoke me!
You haven't invoked me in over forty years!"
I recalled my first trembling toward her and burned with
    shame.

"Beloved," I said, "I didn't want to bother you.
I thought I could say this little on my own,
the way it happens to us in our smallness."

She touched a chord and was herself again—
I have never seen her more glorious—then leaned down
to read what I had written, then stood tall.

"See for yourself what comes of that!" she said,
and struck her lute and was gone wherever she goes
to the silence trembling after her. In silence

I read what I had written, and despaired.
How had I dared imagine I might dare
be only what I am?
                and yet . . .
                        and yet . . .

For Instance

A boy came up the street and there was a girl.
"Hello," they said in passing, then didn't pass.
They began to imagine. They imagined all night
and woke imagining what the other imagined.
Later they woke with no need to imagine.
They were together. They kept waking together.
Once they woke a daughter who got up
and went looking for something without looking back.
But they had one another. Then one of them died.
It makes no difference which. Either. The other
tried to imagine dying, and couldn't really,
but died later, maybe to find out,
though probably not. Not everything that happens
is a learning experience. Maybe nothing is.

Exit Line

Love must intend realities.   —Goodbye.

LIVES OF X

Prologue: Letter to an Indolent Norn

Because they were crude and easy and without fixed
    expectation
    and could, therefore, accept what they got from me,
    interrupting permission only with lashes of temper
    I forgave in rhythm, lashing back
    word for word till the air was striped by our whips,
    and nothing else touched—I thank you, first,
    for the elders of the lost tribe I fell heirless heir to
    and left with no baggage but love, which is weightless,
    a first-day gift of rest in mother and father.

Seven days into the world, two miles from the picnic,
    his head leaking in traffic, his name a skid-mark,
    you broke the man from Sunday, maddened the woman
    all the eighth day jargon of her fears,
    then wasted her witless a long last linger of mush
    crying her veins itched, crying she was a bother,
    crying his lost name fifty years to must, crying
    the expense of nurses would sour me from her,
    then crying from habit, afraid, no longer of something.

And died, I can believe, in an instinct to spare me,
    on just the weekend I happened to be in town.
    From the funeral between two other appointments
    I flew home paid for, not even the travel wasted.
    Was his and hers my payment? "Ma, it's all right,"
    I told her at the last lid to nothing. "It was no bother."

Did you mean me to be glad? There at tribe's crone-cluck,
    whose telling leaked hanged sons like Hell shadow,
    I took you for true dark coming. Were you toying,
    those years you made me mad for God and guilt
    in sweats of prayer, then cut some thread
    and left me bored by my own agonizing? Did
    you cut it? or only break it one day beyond intention,
    yawning and stretching in the slowness of heaven?

For that, and for every chance you missed or made nothing of
    for whatever reason not to be taken for kindness,
    thank you. May all gods come to keep such slovenly ways.

Is mercy no more than the fed hawk's drowse?
But I have been where you fed. I have felt wings,
though never talons. What mercy
is made of oversights? I was brushed and ignored.
When I skidded the road was empty. When I fell
nothing broke. What I loved stayed. It was always
the next plane bloomed black, the next average.
The bomb with my circle in it hit muck and burst buried.
I was grounded by sniffles the day my crew went down.
When the work party was strafed
I was off stealing officers' whiskey, and got it.

I have these wing-tip memoirs, a freak numbering
of chances too zany to bet on. Is that
your game, and rigged? or are you, too, in it,
and losing? However it goes,
thank you. May you stay indifferent
even to my wishing against you, and men
win what they can and lose only at last what they must.

Then I think what games you *have* rigged. Is Harlem,
for instance, your crooked casino? Was Dachau?
Is India so pure a profit you have moved there?
At your sub-headquarters in the black homosexual
who claimed he contracted a habit while writing his book,
the walls were clawed to bone-lath, the chairs
were Spanish Maidens, the air was fishhooked full
of a dust that cut lungs. He screamed toward the lucidity
of an accomplished madness, and you
broke his game with a coughing fit. He fell
frothing and choking, his book a plaid of welts.

At tea in your rest home at the Happy Hilton
the woman with the tattooed wrist came giggling in mink,
played Lady Frolic through two drinks, then screamed.
What ghost had you sent? Her husband cooed her,
swaying.
The house doctor needled her still.
The room gaped oblivions the orchestra blared at,
trying to drown in noise an alp of silence.

At your branch office in the Indian importer
who spoke glass British chipped by American slang,

138

the dice were pure tusk, ruby spots flush to bone.
"The price of famine," he said, holding a lace.
His terrible bargains he knew how to bargain
needled the fingers that touched them. "Lovely,"
the woman said. "Dirt cheap," he smiled.

Well, thank you for good enough in a bad market.
I have suffered nothing I could not bear,
pity and not be made to bear. I have watched losers
look up from the last roll, stunned open,
plungers who came high-rolling and stayed to sweat down
to blood bets marked for broke: a road gang of lepers
who died a game ago or forever, begging bread to gamble,
blood to write home in, bone to cut spots on;
hags in Harold's alley whining to go down for five, two,
anything dice will roll over to stick men
stale on their bones, emptied out of their faces,
motioning, saying the words. In my fevers I hit;
grown cool, I played edges and nibbles, and won a little.
What sits by addicts and has no habit? Is an observer
a good enough thing? By the old wives of the tribe
at dark foretastes, I'll circle you wary: are these
your double-dealt odds?—to nag me easy
till I claw myself in the guilt of not hurting?
When the wino begs my dollar for the death he wants
and I give what costs me nothing, not even pity
for what I can no more help than he can, are you thinking
you'll hook me there? When children starve through news
and I send mercy the deductible check that will, likely,
make no difference, is that what you riddled,
to snare travelers, of the man who died immune?

It won't work. I guess you. I am not indifferent. Yours
is the one mercy by indifference. Mine
is given and taken. I expected less than I have come to
and can give more than I meant.
                                        Besides,
I have died once, knew I would die, knew
it would make no difference; but lived,
and found I had been paid for. Lazarus rights:
can all heaven imagine the ecstacy of first water
down the throat of the dead man risen? what it rinses?

139

what hymns in a sniff of moss? what practice
a dead man's love is? Somehow,
in a movie run backwards, a bomb implodes, soars
from the man's refitting and, in heaven again, starts over
and down in another sequence where being itself
is joy itself and sings for charred brothers
of the first film, too dirty to wish again.

Luck is an innocence: guiltless, I go free; or was guilty,
met law enough, and need none now. I will bear
what I must, ask nothing to bear, and may you
sleep on the numbers till the numbers sleep.
In your whim is our peace. May nothing prompt it
from any indolence that will do for mercy.

The Shaft

At first light in the shadow, over the roach
like topaz on the sill, over the roofs,
the Old North Church spire took its time to heaven
where God took His to answer.
                              I took my drink
at clammy soapstone round a drain of stinks
and slid back into bed, my toes still curled
from the cold lick of linoleum. Ma was first,
shaking the dead stove up. Then Pa,
a rumble hocking phlegm. When the cups clattered
I could get up and climb him and beg *biscotti*
while Ma sipped cups of steam and scolded love.

The shaft went down four darks from light to light,
through smells that scurried, from the sky-lit top
where I built cities of kindling, to cobbly streets
that curved away as men go, round their corners,
to what they do after they kiss their sons.
Where *did* he go? He kissed me and went down,
a step at a time, his derby like a bob.
And then pulled under. And the day begun.

Later, when days were something that had names,
I went there with her, out of my sky-lit first
on the top landing, to the falling streets.
The stores were cellars and they smelled of cheese,
salami, and olive brine. Dark rows of crates,
stacked back to damp brick where the scurries were,
made tunnels in whose sides the one-eyed beans
were binned so deep I could lose all my arm
into their sliding buttons. In a while
I got my cookie and knew I had behaved.
Then up the shaft again, through its four darks
to the top landing where we lived in light.
A latched-on fence playpenned a world I made
of slant and falling towns. Until his derby
rose from the shaft and all the kitchen steamed.

God's cellar was one more dark. A tallow deep
where nickels clinked at racks of burning flowers.
Black shawls kneeled there whispering to the dead,
and left the prayer still burning when they rose.
He had such gold saints by Him in His dark:
why was God so dusty? Was He making
the dead from dust again because she prayed
and made me pray? Would all the dead be made
back to the shawls draped on those altar rails,
and come home singing up their shafts of dark?

I kissed the stone he changed to in his flowers.
But when he stayed away she would not waste
the prayers she lit but got him back in me.
His letters came. From God and Metropolitan.
A piecemeal every week. And he had bought us
half a house in Medford—out of the shaft
and into green that had a river through it.

And still he would not come back, the garden summer
nothing to him, the fruit with nothing to say.
My aunt and uncle bought the other half.

God had a house there, too, but would not speak
His first Italian to her. She came home
and spoke the rest to Pa, hissing all night
how much she was afraid. Or a dream rattled

and speared her to a scream, and the girls woke crying,
and ran to fetch her water, while I lay
guilty of happiness, half-deep in books,
learning to guess how much hysteria
could be a style of acting, and how much
have its own twisted face, and how much more
could be the actress acting what she was,
panting and faint but gripping the glass of water
they always ran to fetch and watch her drink
till she sank back exhausted by medication
and let herself be fussed to sleep again,
satisfied as long as she was feared for.

So all was well. And if a glass of water
and the girls' fears were medicine enough,
why the girls would wake, the pipes would not run dry.

I lost her, and I lost them, shutting out
more night-rattling and more day-squalls
than I had sky for, there behind my books.
I made a cave of them and crept inside
and let the weather blow away unheard.

They had to run those weathers of the dark
forked day and night by lightnings of her nerves.
Not they, nor I, guessed half those howling years
the lightnings were her staff and they her sheep
to frighten close, all madness being fear.

And still they grew away because they grew.
And she came stalking after like a witch
when they strolled after supper. They found her out,
flitting from tree to tree with the black cat
of sniffed suspicion sliding at her feet,
a shadow in a shadow, and they led her
foot-blistering hikes through nowhere and back home,
slowing to let the shadow flit away
around the corner, slide into the house,
be dumped in a back closet, and not be there
to mar her innocence when she looked up
from sorting sorted socks at the kitchen table,
or sweeping the swept floor, and breathing hard,

but half believing their straight-faced innocence
as they clacked by to shut a bedroom door
on gales of whispering with giggly showers.

I read my book and guessed and didn't care.
An oaf in a madhouse. Keeping my escape
but staying on for meals. She learned at last
suspicion makes sore feet. But she wasn't finished.
Not while she still could faint and not come to
till everyone was crying in a circle
of guilt and glasses of water and grand opera.
I didn't know she was crazy. That we all were.

Nor that I dropped my book and lost my place.
I knew she had fainted and we were to blame.

Then, one night when the girls had invitations
her black cat hissed at, she stood in the doorway
ranting to turn them back, and when they argued,
she turned her eyes up, started breathing hard
and settled to the floor across the sill.
She had her act so polished by that time
she could sink like a dropped sheet, all one motion
and down without a thud. It was well done—
It took me in and sent me running for water—
but by whatever tells truth to the badgered,
it was too well done. When I came running back,
the girls had clucked her gently to one side,
pillowed her head, smoothed on a comforter,
and bent to kiss her cheek, cooing, "Poor Ma.
A nap will do her good." And off they clattered,
squeezing their giggles tight. Then even I—
the oaf of the litter—got it. I found the glass
still in my hand, started to put it down,
then drank it off. And, having watched that much,
sat down to watch the rest.
                              Were her eyes closed?
The girls' heels clicked across the porch and off it.
The last click jerked her upright in a rage,
but to one side, in case the girls looked back.
She hadn't seen me and I guessed she meant
to be found lying there when the girls came home.

143

God, what a weapon! I could *hear* her glower,
her lips grimacing vows to kill a saint.
"Have a good nap?" I said.
                                    She snapped around,
head and body together in one shriek.
My skin crawled on a rasp of shame too late.
Then she was on me like her blackest cat,
its claws turned into fists. She beat so hard
it hurt me not to hurt. She'd hurt herself
unless I stopped her. Well, I'm an actor, too,
from a family of actors, I told myself,
and tried to clown it away. "Hey, Ma, lay off.
You'll hurt your wrist again. Come on, let's dance!"
The thing was to catch her mood and turn it around.
I picked her up—she weighed about ten pounds—
waltzed her across the room, her fists still going,
then settled her soft as dandelion fuzz on cushions.
"Just like your father, pig!" she tried to scold,
but her glower was out.
                                    "So what? So it didn't work.
So now you can stop fainting. So what's lost?—
your stage career? It was a lousy act."

I'd kept my head just far enough above books
to guess my best chance was to play her husband.
"Just like your father," she scowled, but her grimace
quivered halfway to a smile. I thought I'd won.
But it slipped past a smile, turned into a giggle,
and out through a mad laughter to a scream
that had no actress in it but the fear
I was no husband to, and could not be.

—And gasped at last, since comedy is all,
to hiccups that went on until she lay
where comedy is nothing, strewn like lint
blown down into the bottom of a well
I could remember like the smell of tallow
inside a dark where racks of burning flowers
swallowed black shawls to altar rails of bone
down every turn and landing of the shaft.

144

If God still spoke her language there, I hope
she heard enough to promise her the light
I didn't know how to light her when I tried.

She did ease into age with half a smile
mending inside her. But her eighties raveled.
Her wits went back to muttering, and she sat
hugging a raggedy doll that would not light back
husband or son. And never saw us again
although we came and stood there in the shaft
bringing her pastries that oozed down her chin,
candies we had to wash out of her fist,
and jokes she did not hear the nurses laugh at.
She hugged her final dark to a rag God
who spoke in broken weathers to no wits.
And then we turned my father's grave and laid her
to take her time to Heaven in her last faint.

And there's a life, God knows, no soul would choose.
And if I send love after it, what's that
but one more scurry sounding down the shaft?

The River

By easy stations where time crossed and left
the banks ahead untouched, the river slipped
seven looped miles from springs to a salt mouth,
brackish a good five miles back from flood tide
but rock-fresh all its length into an ebb.

A cumulus of elm- and maple-green
was every summer, the heaven of it pierced
by a white-slatted Congregational spire
four-sided, with a clock for every wind.
And every wind and clock a story told.

A stone-fenced tidy Zion of thrift and God
the Congregational saints began there once,
their housefronts white on the hills yet, where I heard
the bells to Concord. In the clattering hour

history most chooses, midnight spurred its horse,
and Paul Revere came pounding at the doors
scarred by his knuckles yet—so I was told,
though only the pure-in-heart, the well-invested,
and eagle scouts dead in the line of duty
can see the scars, not always.
                              Seen, unseen,
the saints rode west and northwest all one night
cross-country from green to green of the elm squares
leaving behind bad sculptures and good law,
enough to fill a countryside of causes.

Every nineteenth of April, though now by day
and with refreshments by the American Legion,
he rides again past children waving flags,
and beats on one door of one house still standing
as it was then, though it's a funeral parlor
these new days, though this day, the half-day
it takes to fill the windows with DARS
in ribboned bonnets and tricorned gentlemen,
the corpse in residence must be wheeled away
and down the elevator to the cold room
till that year's rider clatters round the corner
where the horse van that dropped him at South and Main
waits at High and Winthrop to take him on
to the next house of the next town on his way,
already forgotten by the hoodlum young
storming the Armory for free ice cream
and bottles of what Boston still calls "tonic."

This is what I remember from a first.
A half day taken from the mailman's wake
to let a rider by, and a costumed clatter
over the dead man's interrupted state.
Locked in his cellar, he forecast forever
under whose stairs he would lie long the same
while hats and bonnets changed. That afternoon—
whichever year it was—I did my duty
beside his box in the light they brought him back to
before they wheeled him off again forever.

But first, a hoodlum with my hoodlum pack,
my flag and hand out, screaming with the rest,
I stormed the Armory for the Legion's handout.
And ducked out on him fast among his roses.
He was a good round chuckle every day
he hauled his bag, and every week he left
one more $10 piece of Pa in the slot,
and that was food and drink, and a quick Lord's Prayer
as Ma had ordered, and I could have the river
and he his promises.
                          The rafts and cockles
and leaky tubs I drifted summer through
touched every bank. Water rats quizzed my statue
at holes I knew. Dragonflies hummed me dry.
Alewives ran the flickering of their instinct
under my awe. I scooped them in their seizure
and sat seized in my shell, their slate-blue tremble
a mystery like quicksilver at my bare feet
in the constant inch of water beyond bailing.

Then, like the corpse put by for history's party,
or an undelivered mail, sender unknown,
they came one year and tasted their first water
and turned up the white mushrooms of their bellies
bloated like easy death and scummed with oil
in clots and rafts that stank back to the sea
and came up on the tide, and came and went
a week, ten days, till nothing came again
but a few eels too ugly not to live.

Is there a longer death than rivers die
out of the sainted valleys of their first,
following the mist-blown tribes and their dim totems,
and the congregation of saints beside the water
that came and went, and still came and still went
where black stumps of the rotted shipyards stubbed
the sewer-slimed edges of the rotted river?
Where, through the same green cumulus, the spire
the saints appointed as their arm to God
lifted its four clocks to the rose of winds
that took the captains out past God,
                          down river,

147

clearing Hull point, aslant to Provincetown,
and on to the Azores and Canaries.
Until the Trades grew wicked with their south,
the cargo was still God and Medford Rum,
with barter as it came.
                         But before landfall
on the Gold Coast, God's corpse went into the hold
and chain and shackles rigged them out as slavers
triangling to Jamaica in their stink
to trade what flesh had not gone to the sharks
for kegs of black molasses, and then home,
the hold scrubbed out with soda, God broken out
like a new flag to fly above the Square
where God's distillery waited for the syrup
to start a new firewater its three ways
from God, past God, to God again one Sunday.

Their portraits climb the stairs yet, or look down
from rows of deacons and from the bank's walls—
Nathaniels, Ebenezers, Jonathans.
Burnsided, muttonchopped, full-beavered, shaved,
bone-leathered, paunched, frill-collared, or homespun,
all crossed with a gold chain from which time hangs
to take out or put back as the trade turns.

Back to the Sundays when the sloops and barks
wove lines above the chimney tops, the wharves
silent, the gray dray horses out to pasture,
not hearing how the bells poured down from God
to call the Captain's carriage from the hill,
its two spang chestnuts, polished like new boots,
clopping between the pickets, and his Priscilla
bonneted prim but shawled in Indian silk—
a trophy from her trophy home to God
from mysteries of his untold own, but home,
a proper man and propertied and a deacon
with the white house still growing on the hill,
sprouting a new farm after every voyage.

God took them in. His minister at the door
came forward to honor him home, such blessings
He brings us once again from the main deep

148

to the good farms of the righteous. As one by one,
from offstage in themselves, squires with their ladies
passed, tipping their toppers, and God took them in
through the arched door, His portrait rayed above,
fingering the great gold chain from which time hangs.

And cleared his throat—a peal of organ sound—
when all but the tied horses swishing flies
had gone in from the Square and shut the door
on the concluded world with its beasts left over.

Sun in the morning. The river's grenades of light
blinding the ripples. Cock's matins sung. The crows'
black souls, like monks from a grimoire,
scudding back to their hills of warlock oaks.
A lamb bleating its last lawn before Easter—

When I left the river I could walk all day
inside one captain's name. The miles of farms
and tangled woodland his. Ebenezer Hutchens—
master at twenty, owner at twenty-four,
banker at twenty-seven. He died white
and dry as a peeled oak in his blind eighties,
whose bark and beard of youth had known the crows
from more hells than the congregation counted,
but owned the valley on both sides of the river
west of the Square and spire, and the crows' hills
north to the town line through the granite knobs
with black ponds, grubbed with leeches, in their shadows,
seeping to fern and deadfall where a day
blushed Indian pipes, white trillium, lady's-slippers
from bark- and moss-rot of cool bottoms,
the scrub untouched there from the first of saints
into that country.
                        Sun in the morning
to a pine-wood dusk over blueberry clearings,
I walked that one name, rounding its farms like ponds
in the wood shadow. At the Seven Hills,
its white cliff in the last light on the highest,
the Captain's House looked down on the toy spire
that was his boundary stake in the spread valley.
The ships were gone. The river dead. The wharf,

a coalyard drab with barges. The distillery,
blue-lawed to virtue once the trade had ended.
Molasses came from Boston.
                                    A smoke from Sumter
signaled the Hutchenses, Bradfords, Woollseys
to the hot-running Gettysburgs of the righteous.
Even without trade, courage is a cause
and spills its blue boys long to the larks of God.

Old men of the GAR came out to march,
battle flags clearing the way for Paul Revere
every nineteenth of April. But on the hill
in 'forty-seven, Captain Ebenezer,
hunched at his desk of Honduran ironwood,
could tell a future. When abolitionist ladies
called in hymn-singing virtue to petition
against The Trade, and, thinking still as housewives,
complained that slave-ships stank—as if bad odor
were the offense of evil—Ebenezer
unhunched an instant, raised a Captain's head
out of his ruin and answered to first causes:
"Yes, ladies, slavers stink, but money don't."

And was dead himself before one son changed odor
under McClellan's nose, though well downwind
in the smallpox ghettos of the Potomac. Still
one son stormed Mobile and came home with contacts
that were no harm to trade. And another jingled
high Washington among desks that lost nothing
when money was to be made in the Sutlers' Peace.

The Armory took his name beside the river.
An outlet from its boilers steamed all winter
just at the waterline to let me dream
I knew a secret hot spring to the center
and walked on caverns hung with diamond darks.
While in the Armory's groins the Hutchens Light Guard
rattled the rifle range, shouted its numbers,
or changed to West Point uniforms on ball nights
and danced with lady-shadows past the windows
of the upper vault, my eyes glued to the light
that danced away and came and danced and came.

150

It was my country and a mystery sung
by bird, by brook, by squirrels chattering,
and shadows through the trees and old lies told
and histories tipping truths. The stone-farmed hills
hand-labored to their falling pasture walls
let fall a stone a season from their ruin.
The town was the invader. Dying barns
backed half the houses to a picket fence
and apple trees. Great bones of hand-chipped granite
trimmed off the squires' lawns, topped with iron fences.
Cellar walls three feet thick, with every block
of fieldstone a day's labor for two men,
bore oak-pegged beams, like ark work, or found money
building its city firm. But still the cows
roamed to the edge of pavement, and the weeds
poked through a cellar-hole that blotched half the Square,
where the first inn and first stage out from Boston
had rambled till its fire. And still the river
slipped easy as its first from the drowned boys
of summer at their play in sight of farms,
the clay pit, and the old wharf peppered black
where once molasses leaked a bait for flies
in the droning summer from the first, not long.

Then like a traffic's roar Boston spilled out,
first Irish, then Italian. A field at a time
the land went out. The Captain's house came down,
steam shovels ate his lawns, grazed his hills flat
for diagrams of two-by-fours drawn up
a day at a time and hammered shut, roofed, boarded,
given their doors, and left to find a name
with twenty years to pay at six per cent.
The Captain's bones flowered open to his grandsons
in vaults of promised paper with such names
as the valley had not spelled in all its time,
but still could add
                    payable to the order
of the Estate of Ebenezer Hutchens
a Bond and Mortgage covenanted with
Sean Flaherty and said estate to wit:
Aram Perunian and said estate to wit:

Carminantonio Ciardi and said estate
revised to Concetta Ciardi, widow, to wit:
that the lands and bounds and premises hereinafter
together with etc. heretofore
of the Estate of Ebenezer Hutchens
—pay off their life time or return to wit,
whose name, come off the land, returns to it.

A life. And better traded than for molasses.
My father traded his for four hundred weeks
of the $10 checks from Metropolitan.
Two mailmen died before his mail stopped coming.
I think my mother thought they were pallbearers
the government kept sending in his honor.
She liked wakes, and held one for every check
before she sputtered her slant name on the back
and wept it out for food. She knew some wrong
was being done her but was not sure which
and stayed suspicious on principle. Were we wronged?
our piece of a slaver's acre black with blood?
The tales I knew were old and wonderful.
Old and therefore wonderful. Old and dying.

And I was young and happier than her tears
could change me from. The filthy river slipped
smooth as its first. And all one prowling summer
when Will Howe got a job, I had day dibs
on his canoe, a leakless Indian legend
so tremblingly beyond my hammered sticks
that I could stroke the two miles to the Lakes
and prowl the pinefringe sure of mocassin tracks
under the bracken, or cut straight across
the mile-wide water further than the world,
unwronged by any day, in my own country,
whose dead I haunted and whose dead I am.

A Knothole in Spent Time

I have to believe it's a limited society
that remembers the Craddock School on Summer Street
where the tennis courts are now. Still, everyone
is local to his own ghosts. The one-room school
my wife rode spavined Josh to in Haw Creek
hid itself in a thicket for twenty years
after the school bus came, and then was sold
to Mr. Buster Robinson, who moved it
onto his place to house the hired man's family,
and let the thicket back over the well,
the two caved-in outhouses, the skip-rope yard,
the knocked-in stones no memory could sit long on,
though we strolled back for one that wasn't there.

A week before we were married we went down
and found the thicket onyx'd with blackberries,
went back again with a pail and picked it full,
ate them in cream so thick it wouldn't pour
but had to be spooned off the top of the pail.
Alas, the jewel thickets had been threaded
with poison ivy. Judith's arms went scaly.
She had to add long gloves to her wedding gown.
Then, when we took the Pullman to Chicago
the air conditioner quit and we lay sweltering
in a Black Hole of Calcutta. I caught a cold.
And all our honeymoon she scratched, I sniffled.
Our gem days in a sweet too thick to pour.

Are tennis courts a better end than thickets
that poison with their sweets? The elms came down
to let a pavement in. All change unghosts
something we change in leaving. Imagine Wordsworth
revisiting Yarrow—or Tennyson, Locksley Hall—
tourists to a nostalgia (why else go back?)
finding the place scrubbed out to Super Mkts,
cloverleaf ramps, and ten Drive-In Self-Service
Omnimats—they'd suffer a change of style
before they got the poem out of their dendrites
and into itself. I'm doing what they'd have done

at some last elmtop down from heaven's first
not for nostalgia but for nostalgia rebuffed.
My own, but a condition of us all
at the gates of lost infinities.
                                    Craddock School
was hardly an infinity, but could spell one.
As anything begins. My mother took me
my first day gone into its creaking ark;
the huger, I have to guess, for my being small,
but huger again for all Ma's sermoning
on the sanctity and omniscience of school teachers,
as witness their salaries—almost as much as a cop's.
They were born in enormous palaces called "college"
and came to earth in kindness, that small boys
might "get an education" and "get ahead"
as nobody's parents had been able to,
which is why they were "sacrificing." At least why she was.

Which meant she'd strap me if I didn't behave.

Which meant, in the sad nonsense that speaks dearest,
she loved me and feared for me.
                                    In I went.
It's out of focus now. I remember the elms,
a whispering sky that spattered sunlight through,
walls like the sides of a ship, and the ark roof
riding the elms in a sunlight of its own.
It must have been built soon after the Civil War
when lumber still grew on trees and was meant to be used
a tree to the ridge, a half tree to the joist.
It must have taken a forest for the studs.
Even on brightest days the hallway ceilings
were lost in their own dusk. It smelled of chalk,
the furnace room, and sneakers. It creaked and breathed
as if there were giants sleeping in its attics.
If heaven needed a barn for better beasts
than any of us were, the Craddock School
would have done for Apollo's cattle.
                                    I sat down,
pure in worship, ready to be saved,
and even to earn salvation. Miss Matron-Column
(I don't remember her name but she stood pillared

154

over our heads like a corseted caryatid
spilling out of her corsets on a scale
of two of anyone's mother) said what she said,
I don't remember what. I was having trouble.

Ma meant the day to be ritual, and had made me
a jumper-something called a Buster Brown,
and bought me new school shoes, and long white stockings
that buttoned, or tabbed, into my underwear.
I wasn't exactly comfortable but I took it
until a pug-nosed Irish snot behind me
—Tom something-or-other—got his needle in
to let me know white stockings were for girls
and that I was not only a Dago but a sissy.

I had set out to worship and be saved.
Now I'd have to fight when school was out.
The fight wouldn't be much, but it meant ripped buttons,
probably grass stains, maybe a red-lined nose,
and that meant Ma and the strap. I was better off
when I ran into trouble on troubled days.
But when the day began in a fuss of love
and then went sour, that meant I had betrayed her.
Which meant our opera played with the volume up
screaming to extra whacks with that damned strap.

While I was thinking that, I was looking around:
most of the girls, alas, had on white stockings
and none of the boys. The stinker saw me looking,
knew he had me, and began recruiting
more of the boys. Why did God have to waste
good schools on the lousy Irish?
                                    —I heard a name.
"John Sea-YARD-i," Miss Matron-Column said,
"are you sure you are paying attention?"
                                    I sat up
and tried to manage the look I guessed she wanted,
but I had forgotten even the stink behind me:
Omniscience had changed my name! I was John Sea-YARD-i
—and not even allowed to argue! What's a teacher
if she can't say a name right? . . . John Sea-YARD-i . . .
That was no sound of mine. I was John CHAR-di.

I knew that. And Ma knew it . . . well, what *did* Ma know?
House things, yes. And things about Italy.
But nothing about what went on out of the house,
such as how to say an American name in America.

I had been rechristened. All the way through high school
and my little while at Bates and my time at Tufts
—at both of which there were kids I'd started school with—
I was Sea-YARD-i. It took me seventeen years
and a bus ride out to Michigan—out past Canada—
to make my escape. And the first thing I did, free,
was to get rid forever of Matron-Column's
last ghost upon me and get my own ghost back
the way it sounded when its ghost began.

Meanwhile, to keep insanity in sequence,
we had our fight. I bloodied my jumper a fleck,
lost the buttons I expected to lose,
got grass stains on my knees. We tried our cuss words,
then backed off trading sneers and started home.

Ma would be waiting with that strap. My tail
would come away from it ridged. Then *she'd* cry,
and I would have to stop bawling to comfort *her.*
I've never thought far enough back—not for not trying—
to understand how we came to that arrangement.
I know it had something to do with my being ghosted
into her husband and he into her son.
Sometimes I think she was beating him for dying,
and me for not being enough of what she'd lost.

Something like fifty years later, when she'd faded
almost past touch and hearing in the Home,
but was still half remembering who we were
when we went to visit, and then forgetting again—
her long ghosts out, back in her ghosts again,
I sat beside her and she called me "'Ndo."
("'Ndo" was her way of shortening "Antonio.")
What visitation in what mist was that?
Not he. Not I. A ghost halfway to black.
Then she drew back through mists I could not enter
even as a ghost.
                    Which year of what came first?

156

Time's all one once it's by. The ghost I walked in
was scheming its small way out of a ridged butt.
"Look what you did!" I yelled when I slammed in.
—If I could stake my claim as the offended
before she staked her own, I had a chance.
"These are GIRL stockings! I had to fight ALL the boys!"
(I never was stingy with flourishes. This was opera.)
"They called me a GIRL and tried to rip my stockings!"

I doubt it would have worked, all else being equal,
but my sister Edie came home just then from her school
full of hot news. "Ma, Johnny had a fight!"
she yelled, and waited around to see me get it.

Ma shut her up. *"Fati i cazzi tui!"*
—that's mountain barnyard Billingsgate, southern style,
for "mind your own phallic business." When Ma got earthy
she never was one to mind a little manure.
Except in recollection, those nine lives back,
I wouldn't even have noticed, except to know
I was off the hook once she shut Edie up.
"Take off the stockings," she sighed her martyrdom.
And when I had them off she tossed them to Edie.

"Somebody has to wear them," she said. "Go wash them.
—And you: get out of those clothes so I can fix them."

I changed to overalls and went back to the kitchen.
"Ma, the teacher said I was John Sea-YARD-i.
That's not our name."
                        "Che nomi! First your sisters—
now you. *Chi ne capisce?* Say what you like."
Then she caught herself: "You do what the teacher says."
I shrugged and started out. She called me back.
"I'm sorry about the stockings. I didn't know.
You want a *tarallo?"* (That's a hard shell bagel.)
"That's all right," I said. But I took the *tarallo.*

That did for my first day into omniscience.
I settled down to worship as I was told,
and wouldn't have thought not to. I learned to write "Squirrel"
with a bushy tail on the "q," "Look" with two eyes,
"Cat" with a whiskery "C"—proofs of a heaven

157

where things were locked forever in their names
as Nona and every Old Wife knew already
and could mumble charms for; as my Uncle Alec
could lay *tarrochi* pictures out of the deck
and read the next thing coming, that always turned out
to be something else, that on re-examination
turned out to be what the cards had really said
except that he'd read them wrong. The cards and teachers
(and, later, Mussolini) were always right.

I doubted the cards, and never took Mussolini
for heaven's hope, but of the omniscience of teachers
I was God-certified and rebaptized
in perfect faith—at least for one more year.
Then I found my first knothole in spent time.

I had been passed along from Miss Matron-Column,
Sea-YARD-i'd and still in awe, to Miss Absolute Void.
Don't take that name for disparagement: I was still
ready to play *cherubino* to all God's virgins
in our first age of innocence, but the fact is
I haven't a shred of her in my memory
except that she was the first chink in the wall
of heavens I had been schooled to as a faith,
though she didn't know it, and couldn't have been told.
I doubt she could have guessed the wall was there.

I droned fly-drowsy sun its leafy day
down through the elm's own daydream into mine.
The class was reading something, each in turn
rising to take a page—some Henny-Penny
or Puss in Boots. I'd read it twenty times,
and was off somewhere through elmtops in a float
when green clouds split to thunder. "John Sea-YARD-i,"
she called, her voice a judgment waiting to fall.
The book was on my desk but I'd lost the page.
I got to my feet. Somewhere in a separate haze
I remembered a girl reading and her last words
still floating in the elmtops. I held the book
and said from memory whatever Blind Mice
or Chicken-Little came next, pretending to read,
and knowing I'd make a slip, and read forever,

and DIDN'T make one! I must have been twelve years old,
having begun at six, before I heard,
"Very well, then. You may sit. And pay attention!"
I sat, relieved at first. Then burst inside:
I'd fooled her! She thought I had been reading! She was a
    Teacher
and *I* had fooled *her*! I started to tell the kid
ahead or behind or beside me or all at once.
Then hit on a truth as if I'd cracked my skull—
they wouldn't believe me! Ma wouldn't understand.
My sisters wouldn't care. Miss Absolute Void—
well, how could I tell her? I was alone
my first time into the world, at an edge of light
that dizzied like a dark; my gloat, half fear,
my eye at its first peephole into heavens
where Teachers were only people and could be wrong,
and all Ma's stations and candles could be rounded
by a truth I'd caught and held, and couldn't tell!

Thirty years later I did tell Merrill Moore,
though it was half a joke then. A slick squad
of thugs had cracked the Brink's Express in Boston
for the biggest haul in history, and over lunch
Merrill was theorizing they had to be caught
in spite of what seemed to be the perfect crime.

"Give them a year—or two—or three," he said.
"They're sitting on a world's record and can't claim it.
The money's cached: they wouldn't dare start spending.
Meanwhile they have to act as if nothing had happened.
Which is to say they're still bums among bums.
How long can a hero play at being a bum?
Some tart will give a man his walking papers,
a bar will shut off credit, a drunk will laugh.
Can a champion's ego hide in rags forever?
Ego's a king, and kings must claim their crowns."

"Maybe," I told him, "but what if you know to start with
no one will believe you while it still matters?"
And I told him how I'd found my hole in heaven
and seen Miss Absolute Void take off her wings
and soak her feet in a bucket of steaming water,

159

and never found a heaven whole again
nor anyone to tell about what I'd found.

"Well," Merrill said, "the Brink's Boys have the cash
to prove their story, wherever they have it hidden."

And so they had. I hadn't even the building
I could go back to and say, for whatever good
nostalgia of place might do me, "This is the room.
The first place in the world where I was alone
with more than I could tell of what was true.
Here something-nothing happened, and I remember
the day, the place, its ghost of elm-light falling,
and that I went through a door that wasn't there,
except that it once was real, and now it isn't."

And what is, but this lingering back of ghosts?

Feasts

My Uncle Alec's friend, Dominic Cataldo,
was straw boss of the treetop monkey gang
at Forest Hills, the woodpark cemetery
just at the edge of Boston. Across the street,
the North End's dead were tenemented tight
right to St. Michael's fence, stone crowding stone
and four names to a slab, but at Forest Hills,
down maple-dappled rhododendron drives,
the dead kept their suburbias lawned and sloped
to birdy hedges, brooklets, squirrel chatter,
and pheasant dells where dawn mist looked like snow.

St. Mike's looked like Pompeii on market day,
which must have looked like Prince Street excavated
after the stalls and pushcarts turned to stone
around the soot-streaked angels who froze there
in the act of reaching down to feel a melon
they never would pick up to bargain for.

The dead, like the Etruscans, kept their houses,
their neighborhoods, and their uses whole to God,

160

still zoned by ordinance. On Memorial Day,
a slope down from the villas of still money,
St. Mike's was at death's rush hour, the commuters
all carrying lunch and stiff wax wreaths to stone
past red-hot ice-cold hawkers. I planted pansies
I brought from home to border a last house,
prayed, ate my lunch, and spilled an orange tonic
that wet Pa's granite name, and prayed for that,
though it couldn't be a sin. I hadn't meant it.
I didn't even have another nickel
and had to drink tap water, iron-flavored.

Ma drank her tears awhile, then stilled to prayer,
then stood me by her in the receiving line,
her husband's name to her right, and sighed through neighbors,
cousins, *paesani*, and the delegation
from the Sons of Italy with its three-foot wreath
slant-ribboned *Presidente e fratello*—
Eterno in noi il santissimo ricordo.

It was her last of matronage, the one house
where she could stand, her husband at her side,
and welcome in the man's guests. All year long
she waited for that afternoon of graces,
once more a wife and ritual to his name
and presence. And all the loud hour on the El
and the half more on the trolley back to Medford
she sat carved straight to a found etiquette
she hadn't meant to lose, though late that night
I'd wake to hear her fear hiss through its dreams.

Still I passed Pa's grave more times than I stopped.
I spent more Sunday mornings at Forest Hills
than at St. Mike's. Which brings me to Cataldo,
to Uncle Alec, and to being bird dog
for the last organized gang of pheasant poachers
to operate within the city limits
of Boston, Mass; a gang led by Cataldo,
a long-armed, bow-legged, broken-toothed gorilla
with a chest of hair that coiled up like black smoke
from open collar to jawbone, and who was known
through all the bellowed treetops as Sputasangue,

161

which means "Spitblood," and was the heave-ho cry
he gave his sweaty gangs when backs were breaking
at crowbars and at peaveys and needed a lash
to break the boulder from the sucking till
or start the felled log over.
                              I rang with joy
whenever Cataldo, halfway down his gallon,
turned into Sputasangue, the one artist
I ever knew to stretch a roaring curse
a full ten minutes and not run out of figures
nor use the same one twice. Religious poetry
lost a fountain the day he was kept from school
to weed his first dry ledge. The man could start
at the triune top and work the hagiography
down to St. Fish by strict anatomizings,
to frottery, battery, buggery, rape, plain mayhem,
and on to atrocious-assault-with-intent, compounded
twelve generations back and twenty forward.

He made me a bull-roarer once and showed me
how I could whirl the thing till the air shook—
Cataldo did. But Sunday nights in the kitchen
when Sputasangue smoked up from the jug,
I sat my corner and heard the vault of glory
split its stone arches and spin heaven and hell
in the avalanche of rhetoric, while Ma shook,
helpless in admiration, and Uncle Alec
bravoed the rhapsode at the root of man,
his flowering tongues.
                         Cataldo died of the shakes
a dry ghost later, but while he was a man,
the goatiest Greek down from the mountaintops
could not outhowl him on God's axletree,
nor chop it down so sighted to a line
that it would crack a walnut but not mash it.

Being half a Greek himself, he was a thief,
which is to say, a mountain fox. Forest Hills
was stocked with ring-neck pheasants that did so badly
in what seemed perfect cover, the hatcheries
had to ship crate on crate, month after month.
Something kept getting at them. Sputasangue

would go to the headman's office with a sack
of feathers, heads, and legs found in the bottoms
where skunks had left them, and would volunteer
to gun the varmints by the Trinity,
the twelve Apostles' crooks, and Lucifer's tail,
if he had to twist if off himself.
                                        That got him
the keys to iron gates. Sundays at dawn,
a throbbing touring car—a rusty Moon
that belonged to my Uncle Alec's friend Joe Pipe-dreams—
coughed through the gates. Uncle and Sputasangue
sat in the back, one shotgun left, one right.
Joe Pipe-dreams drove. I rode in front, cocked ready
whenever I got the signal, to jump out
and stuff the haul into a burlap sack.

Down in the dell, mist dreamed among the grasses
in the first light, and then a pheasant's head
would twitch up from no body like a snake
swimming but head high, half as Milton dreamed
Old Scaleskin for his cakewalk up to Eve
before God, Calvin, and William Jennings Bryan
condemned him to go crawling for the sins
he was already damned for in Tennessee
and the one-book farms of glory.
                                        The old Moon
crawled at two miles an hour, Joe Pipe-dreams working
the spark and choke to make the thing backfire.
That flushed the birds. Then shotguns and backfiring
made one blur, till my uncle gave the word
and I went running with the burlap sack.

Our least haul was sixteen before the mist
drained to full day-ray. Later, Sputasangue
would walk his traps, finish a skunk or two,
and drop it behind the greenhouse for the headman.
Then he would empty the bird sack and twist off
heads, feet, and plucks of feathers in evidence.
He didn't have to be so foxy about it,
but man's the artist of his means. Art served,
we all drove back to Medford and gluttony.

Pipe-dreams and Sputasangue didn't want birds.
Not to take home. If they had a home, and I doubt it.
They played at hen-house fox as an act of nature.
Had the headman kept chickens, they'd as soon
have saved the shotgun shells. Why waste good money?
We didn't hunt: we harvested God's hand
and lived well out of it. As for those two,
they were both bachelors married to sour wine
they reeked of, and Uncle Alec, who made his own
(in the Aladdin's cave of barrels, bottles,
Mason jars, pickled peppers, crocks of lard
with half-fried liver balls layered in to keep,
apple chests drying under hanging herbs,
sausage, and drying grapes, the stacked squashes
by sand bins for potatoes, beets, and carrots,
under the footsteps sounding from the kitchen)
drew off a bottle of his best to start them,
and another when that went dry, and then another,
while Sputasangue made it up to rhetoric,
and Ma and Aunt Christina, back from the fields
with dandelions and mushrooms, plucked the pheasants,
worked up the ovens to roasting, and started sauces
we gorged on for two hours in steams of heaven,
then slept off like a drunk, then woke again
to gorge again the last feast not to die.

Food was the flaming altar of the house.
All Hunger's tribesmen praise God as a feast,
fear him as famine, live as they can between.
Those birds were free grace and our week-long meat.
Hens cost money and were needed to lay,
and killing one cut into capital.
But free birds and free mushrooms sent a steam
up to the holy ghost that shines on harvests.

The stinking hen house and its morning bulbs,
green-smeared by droppings, was another bin.
Another was the garden where I sweated
my spring shame at manure I scooped from streets
and hauled home in a barrow while the fiends
who were my friends leered from the fence, and Riley,
the iceman, stopped his wagon to work me over

and offer me the next plop from his nag
if I would follow him.
                    But the Great Bin
was Albert's farm in Marlboro, twenty miles off
on pavement and ten in ruts, though that Joe Pipe-dreams
would have driven to Anchorage for the gas plus wine.

Every crop in, or when new mushrooms sprouted,
Albert would phone, and while Uncle Alec potted,
in or out of season, God's great day
of squirrels, rabbits, and anything with wings
(a robin in spaghetti sauce was a meatball
that didn't have to be bought) I dug potatoes,
or filled my sacks with apples, pears, and corn,
while Ma and Aunt Cristina worked moss bottoms
of rotten trunks for mushrooms. We drove back
with sacks lashed to the fenders, milk cans rattling
the cheeses Ma would make late, Uncle Alec's
bloodstained knapsack tucked under my feet—
and that was food and faith and holiday
high mounded home in incense of oregano,
basil, parsley, bay, mint, tarragon,
and oils that crisped the body and the blood
of rabbit, squirrel, and of whole small birds
whose skulls we nut-cracked for the brain's sweetmeat
when every bone was picked. Then the house clinked
its dishes and the innocent sat glad,
leftovers shelving a next day's gift of grace
from open-handed heaven, whose clenched fist
had starved the mountain hamlets back to stone
deeper than Pompeii's, whose forgotten tongue
they twisted and still spoke for Heaven's
unanswering name; till sweating at their sacks
stuffed with the last of nothing, they went steerage
to heavens whose last gate was St. Michael's slum—
itself a heaven to which no man went starved.

I diet in suburbias past the dead
on checkbook lo-cal, or, a jet away,
pick at my sirloin among signing angels
who skip potatoes for a third martini.
Poor Alec's 94 and has religion

in both bad legs. He lives on the third floor
of what God left him, where he prays to God
to call him in before his legs give out.
I offered to pay the first-floor rent to spare him
those flights of stairs. He gummed a dunked *biscotto*
and shook his head too late a world away.
Those stairs were the one challenge time had left him.
His whined prayers were the tendons of his climb,
his diet of last dusts before the dead,
half dead already.
            And still I had had my first
hound pup and shotgun from his living hand,
who lived beyond himself, locked forty years
in the shop under the El on Causeway Street,
but climbed his foxy Sundays to the feast
of God's permission to man's appetite,
and cheered on the bull-roarer in his power.

And were I God, and he back in My dust,
and I, in the infinity of My whim,
could give him back his prayers or appetites,
but not both—oh, as foxy as the foxes
I made of My own nature, I'd rig his answer
against the palsied maunder of his end
and send him back to Sunday in his power
over the gift-wrapped morning of the world
to its daylong feast and night-roar up from wine—
My man of plenty, ritual to his friends,
and honored home and hale, safe in the garden
that flowered forever, till it wasn't there.

Romancing with Our Beasts

Hot summer nights a space hum at my window
tweetered from grasses, woofered from gulping muds,
the signals throbbing up through one another
in some insomniac radio's reverie;
while from the Parkway just across the river
tires droned, shrilled, and hummed off, like a mosquito,

166

in three tones past my ear. How many sounds
is one sound? This hummed whistling while it whined
over the simmering wavelengths of the dark.

Outside the house, on this side of the river,
too heavily tuneless for their pitch to change
though they growled near, roared up, and growled away,
trucks from and to New Hampshire rattled South Street
till panes burred and beams muttered in their joints.
A quarter on the dresser rang awake
then droned back to the heaviness of time.

Across the river it was all pleasure traffic.
And in a hurry for pleasure, its tires ringing
speed-smooth macadam, a long shrill up and away
beside St. Joe's and through the Winthrop lights
wherever joyrides go, or drunks to bed,
or high school kids to the moon. When the tires screamed
you could start to count, and if you got to ten
before the *krump*, no one was really hurt.
If it came by five, you'd hear glass crack its bells.
At less than five you could start counting corpses.

It took two minutes, including time for dressing
—half of it on the run—to sprint up South Street,
over the bridge, and across the river meadow
to where the beetle shells lay bashed and oozing,
or flipped dead on their backs with a last reflex
still twitching in them. Or over but still racing,
the wheels gone mad with no weight on their reason
and spinning up to a shrapnel of bad rubber,
sometimes a hail of bouncing meteors,
sometimes lashing a welt across the tank
to let the gas out, fluttering red and blue
like a one-winged butterfly or a Chinese fan
that wavered and collapsed and fell away
to let the dead beast die. If it didn't burn
and roar back higher than cop-lights to the moon.

So—except for burning—one topless monster,
its wheels past governance, lay on its back
flush to the road as if it were a barge

and the road its waterline. Firemen stood by,
brass nozzles aimed but waiting in case whatever
lay in the hold could still breathe. Till a wrecker
long-armed a bar that broke the gas connection,
then crouched astride the shell like a praying mantis
half lifting it, half tenderly, to its jaws,
while cops poked light beams into it, stopped, then signaled
to haul it over and open. And over it went.
Whatever dark it was the box of lit
for all to see—and there was nothing there
but the ghost of one white shoe in the outbound lane.

The wrecker hunched and panted. A red pumper
snorted, then eased its breathing. Cops waved by
the gaping traffic that pulled over and spilled
its tourists among tourists. At one corner
a black accordion sprawled across a drain,
gashed open, its strewn teeth swept back beneath it,
the player's corpse already blanketed
and shelved in the trembling ambulance, still ajar
for heaven and hell.
                    But can souls snatch their corpses
and take off without waiting? Where was this one?
The road was river meadow on one side,
and rotten woods, half swamp-sunk, on the other.
There was nothing on the grass. Cops beat the brush
where the fire truck sent a beam from its red lighthouse
to point the way to nothing in the mud suck.
For nothing. Till the beam slipped or was pointed
into a tree, and there above his hunters
the man lay scrawled, nailed open by a branch
that had to be sawed off to get him down.

What proof of what was I those wailing nights
up running from my sleep before it broke?
I never missed a death for being slow
nor a mangle for being timid. I was there;
the dark's first witness and the next day's news.
I needed every horror I could eat.
Or meant to have it, whatever it was I needed.
How do you keep a boy from being fast
to free disasters? I was the volunteer

168

at every carnage, the disgust of cops
—themselves thrilled with revulsion—who growled me off
but were always satisfied when they had cussed me
two steps back before I took three forward.
They swore that we are guilty of what we are,
and let me stay because I shared their guilt.
We were there in one emotion. Townsmen of it,
where every town has its own corner for it. Ours
was Winthrop and the Parkway—two intents
no traffic light could separate for long
while fools had wheels and nights had far to go.

And I had one more license: half the time
when I was up and running, I made it there
before the cops. There was an acoustic trick
built into the meadow and beamed across the river.
Somehow my window was an amplifier.
Or I was amplified inside myself
to tell by the counted scream, before it happened,
what was about to happen. When I grew older—
when I was home from school and had learned by blood
I needn't run for blood—I'd be on the phone
(we had one in by then) to the desk sergeant
before the echo thudded out. The station
was down the street on Main in a streetcar rumble
outside my echo chamber. In light traffic
a wreck could wait a life out still unfound.
But I could wail the cops there in shrill seconds
and be back to sleep before a ruptured tank
had washed the blood off in the public service.

Not that I ever asked to be death's puppy.
I woke nights being told and did what came,
sniffing revulsions till I'd had my fill
of how a body mangles, and could settle
for dialing mercy, such as it was, to come
and count the pieces, tending what it could.

The last bashed corpse I went to was Mike Flynn's,
and not across the river but wavering home
with God's own skinful picked up God knows where
and crossing South Street when some high-school kid

burned up from Main. I'd watched Mike times enough
come murdering two o'clock outside my window
due North by East-South-West in a looping lurch
from whiskey to a sot's end. He could weather
three yards to either side of a straight line
and three more luffing round to start again,
and call that walking home, and call his gargle
an Irish tenor, were he fit to call.

I heard him come, unreeling Mother Machree
out of a rusty gizzard, and—from nowhere—
one yelp of brakes, and instantly a bludgeon
whacking a bladder, and then the brakes cat-screeching
at least a ten-count after, and a tinkle
on the front porch and off.
                                        I called the cops
before I even looked, then went outdoors,
turning the porch light on. A Model A,
one light still on, and up, its front wheels tilted,
was snagged on Kelly's hedge. On my own steps
I caught a glimmer of nothing that was mine
and picked up a smashed wristwatch with no works—
the case and an expansion band. (Weeks later,
while I was mowing, a blade snagged on a rust
that was a movement rotted out of keeping.
I held it like a chewed coin in my hand
and couldn't think what to think until I thought it
and flipped it into the trash can with dead time.)

Across the street cops were already flashing
where a Greek chorus of neighbors in grabbed wrappers
stage-whispered "Flynn! Mike Flynn!" above the mangle,
the breath still snoring in it, splints of bone
howling outside their flesh and, like a faith,
the reek of whiskey mounting higher than death.
He was so badly knotted on himself
it took a while to see one leg was missing.
Joey Damestri found it on a mallow
broad as a platter among the riverbank weeds,
and one of the cops wrapped the great leaf around it
to lift it toward what sacrament that was.

What ruin was the man? What ruin are we?
I saw, like those pneumatic tubes at Kresge's,
a dark from God's dark hand let this man down
exactly where he lay, his life inclosed
and blown to this one end; and we, like him,
blown there above it, exactly as we were,
choiceless as singing drunks their long dark home,
till we, too, are shed down a bank of weeds.

I gave a cop the watch case and its strap
just as I heard the breath snore up and stop.
Then thought I heard it again. But turned around
and it was the driver blubbering. "Look at him!
Oh, Jesus, look at him!" And then, like God,
or like a flight of His most jeweled angels
out for a fling and wailing as they dove,
the ambulance raved blinking down the dark,
gathered the jostled puzzle of the man
and, solved or not, took off with what it had,
and all was done.
                        And what was done? The boy
got two years for "vehicular homicide
with extenuation" or whatever it was
I half recall from legal idiom, meaning
reform school, but suspended and on probation.
For form's sake, I suppose. He *had* been speeding.
But Mike Flynn, if I knew him, had been swinging
from shadow to shadow. I'm not sure a bat
could have dodged him in his lurches.
                              The neighbors and I
got nothing but a hair caught in our throats,
and the shriek of a sure knowledge that hissed down
to words again, and could be held and stacked
and spilled on grocery counters and pool tables
to prove we were authentic to that death
and had bent over it, gloating like men,
women, and children. Mad in our crouch of lust.
Changing to mercy when we could change back
to the faces we grow long in. But pulled short
those shuddering nights romancing with our beasts,
the rape we wait for in our stalest dark.

The Benefits of an Education:
Boston, 1931

A hulk, three masted once, three stubbed now,
carried away by any history, and dumped
in a mud ballast of low tide, heeled over
and a third swallowed in a black suck
south of the Nixie's Mate—itself going—
gave me a seal of memory for a wax
I wouldn't find for years yet: this was Boston.
Men with nothing to do plovered the sand-edge
with clam rakes that raked nothing. I walked home
over the drawbridge, skirting, on my right,
Charlestown ramshackled over Bunker Hill
and waiting for hopped-up kids to ride The Loop
and die in a tin rumple against the girders
of Sullivan Square, or dodge away toward Everett
and ditch the car; then walk home and be heroes
to ingrown boyos, poor as the streets they prowled.

There, house to house, the auctioneer's red flag
drooped its torn foreclosure to no buyer.
Now and then a blind man who could see,
and his squat wife who could stare out at nothing,
sat on the curb by the stacked furniture
and put the babies to sleep in dresser drawers
till charity came, or rain made pulp of all.
The rest lived in, guarding their limp red flags.
The bank was the new owner and that was all.
Why evict nothing much to make room for nothing?
Some sort of man is better than no man,
and might scrounge crates to keep the pipes from freezing
until the Water Co turned off the meter.
Or come Election, when men got their dole,
the bank might get the trickle of a rent
that wasn't there.
                    I'd walked those seven miles
from Medford to T Wharf to get my job
on the *King Philip*. Well, not quite a job,
but work, free passage, and a chance to scrounge

nickels and fish all summer till school opened
Miss Bates and Washington Irving.
                                    The *King Philip*
rose sheer, three river-boat-decks top heavy;
but she could ride an inner-harbor swell
and not quite capsize, though, God knows, she'd try.

Excursion fishing. She put out at nine
from the creaking stink of Sicilian fishing boats
praying for gasoline they sometimes got.
And came back in at five—in any weather
that might turn up a dollar-a-head half deck-load
doling four quarters into the first mate's hand
as if the fish they meant to eat were in it
and not still on a bottom out past luck.
Sometimes a hundred or more, but of them all
not twenty would turn up with a dollar bill.
It was all change. We called the first mate Jingles,
waiting for him to walk across the wharf
and spill his pockets into the tin box
in the Fish Mkt safe. When he came back
his name was Dixon and we could cast off.
Your dollar bought you eight hours on the water,
free lines, free bait, your catch, and—noon to one—
all the fish chowder you could eat.
                                    Good days,
the decks were slimed with pollock, cod, hake, haddock,
a flounder or two, and now and then a skate.
(A sharp man with a saw-toothed small tin can
can punch out Foolish Scallops from a skate's wing.
A Foolish Scallop is a scallop for fools
who eat it and don't know better.) I made a scraper
by screwing bottle caps to an oak paddle
and went my rounds, cleaning the catch for pennies,
or grabbing a gaff to help haul in the big ones.

Dixon, jingling again, took up a pool—
a dollar for the biggest cod or haddock,
a half for the largest fish of any kind.
No house cut but the little he could steal
and not be caught or, being caught, pass off
as an honest man's mistake in a ripped pocket.

The deal was winner-take-all. And the man that gaffed
the winning fish aboard was down for a tip.

One Sunday, with over a hundred in the pool,
I gaffed a skate we couldn't get aboard.
Dixon boathooked it dead still in the water,
then rigged a sling and tackle from rotten gear
and I went over the side and punched two holes
behind its head. Then we payed out the hooks
the fireman used for hauling cans of ashes
to dump them overboard, and I hooked it on,
and all hands hauled it clear to hang like a mat
from the main to the lower deck. We couldn't weigh it,
but it was no contest. Dixon paid on the spot.
He counted it out to fifty-seven dollars,
and I got two.
                    We took it in to the wharf
and let it hang—a flag—till the next day
when we cut it loose with half a ceremony,
mostly of flies, just as we cleared Deer Island.
The Captain didn't want that shadow floating
over his treasury of likely bottoms,
so we let the current have it.
                    After five,
the fireman rigged the hose, turned on the pressure,
and I washed down, flying the fish and fish guts
out of the scuppers in a rainbow spray
to a congregation of God-maddened gulls
screaming their witness over the stinking slip.
For leavings.
                    Fishermen are no keepers. One to eat,
a few to give away, and that's enough.
The scuppers might spill over, and the deck
on both sides of a walkway might be littered
with blue-backed and white-bellied gapers staring.

I cleaned the best to haul home. Or I did
when I had carfare, or thought I could climb the fence
into the El and ride free. Now and then,
Gillis, who ran a market next to ruin,
would buy a cod or haddock for nothing a pound
and throw in a pack of Camels.

                          And half the time
an old clutch of black shawl with a face inside it
and a nickel in its fist would flutter aboard
like something blown from a clothesline near a freight yard,
and squeeze a split accordion in her lungs
to wheeze for a bit of "any old fish left over,"
flashing her nickel like a badge, and singing
widowed beatitudes when I picked a good one
and wrapped it in newspaper and passed it over
and refused her ritual nickel the third time.

"I can afford to pay, son."
                                    "Sure you can."
"Here, now, it's honest money."
                                    "Sure it is."
"Well, take it then."
                          "Compliments of the house."
"God bless you and your proud mother,"
she'd end, and take the wind back to her line.
Then the Fish Mkt man got after Dixon
for letting me steal his customers. Nickels are nickels:
for all he knew, I might be stealing from him
out of that pocket of nothing. But I foxed him.
Next time the old shawl came I sent her off
to wait by Atlantic Avenue. (And I'm damned
if the Fish Mkt man didn't call to her
waving a flipper of old bloat, calling "Cheap!
Just right for a pot of chowder!") After that,
I made an extra bundle every night,
cleaned and filet'd, and when she wasn't there
I fed the cats, or anything else of God's
that didn't run a market.
                          Then five nights running
she didn't come. Which, in God's proper market
might be more mercy than all nickels are,
whoever keeps the register, whoever
folds old shawls for burial.

                          Some nights—
once, twice a week, or some weeks not, the ship
was chartered for a stag by the VFW,
(we used to call them the Victims of Foreign Whores)

                                                        175

or some lodge, or some club, though the promoter
was always the same stink in tired tout's tweed.
He rigged a rigged wheel forward on the lower deck.
Sold bootleg by the men's room. Used the Ladies'
as an undressing room for the girlie show
that squeezed its naked pinched companionway
to the main deck "salon" to do the split
or sun itself in leers, clutching a stanchion,
or, when the hat was passed, to mount the table
and play house, if not home, two at a time,
with a gorilla stinking of pomade
who came on in a bathrobe from the Ladies'.
Two shows a night, prompt as mind's death could make them
while it still had a body. And on the top deck,
for an extra quarter, Tillie the Artist's Model
undid her flickering all on a canvas screen
lashed to the back of the wheelhouse, where the Captain
kept a sharp Yankee watch for the Harbor Cruiser.

He was a good gray stick of salt, hull down
in some lost boyhood that had put to sea
with the last whales still running into myth.
And down to this, or be beached flat, keeled over
like Boston, or that hulk off the Nixie's Mate,
to stink in the mud for nothing.
                                   Nevertheless,
It was some education in some school.
I panted at those desks of flesh flung open,
did mountains of dream homework with willing Tillie,
and, mornings, ran a cloth and a feather duster
(God knows where it came from—I'd guess Mrs. Madden
who cooked the daily chowder of leftovers
in her throbbing galley) over the counters, chairs,
and the great ark-built table, still flesh-haunted.

If it wasn't an education, it was lessons
in something I had to know before I could learn
what I was learning. Whatever there was to learn
in the stinking slips and cat-and-rat wet alleys
off the black girders and the slatted shadow
of the Atlantic Avenue El in Boston
where the edge-grinding wheels of nothing screeched

something from Hell at every sooty bend
of the oil-grimed and horse-dolloped cobbles
from Federal Street to the West End's garlic ghetto,
where black-toothed whores asked sailors for a buck
but took them for a quarter, in the freight yards,
or on the loading platforms behind North Station,
or in any alley where the kids had stoned
the street lights to permission.
                I took home
more than I brought with me of all Miss Blake
and Washington Irving knew of Sleepy Hollow.
(It had stayed clean and leafy I discovered
years later—like the Captain's boyhood
waiting its fo'c'sle south of Marblehead—
yet, a day further on the same road West,
the hollows had turned grimy, and the hills
fell through tipped crowns of slag—like Beacon Hill
stumbling through trash-can alleys to Scollay Square.)

Still, I got one thing from my education.
One stag-night when the tired tout's bootleg sold
too well for what it was, four poisoned drunks
lay writhing in the stern on the lower deck
in their own spew. And one, half dead but groaning,
green in his sweat, lay choking and dry-heaving,
his pump broken. While from the deck above
girls clattered, the pimp spieled, and the crowd raved.

Dixon came after me with the tout. "Hey, kid,
got a good stomach?" Dixon said. "Yeah, sure,"
I told him, honored.
                "It's a dirty job."
"What isn't?"
                "Five bucks!" said the tout. "Five bucks!
Here, Johnny. Five bucks cash and you can hold it!
My God, the guy could *die*!"—and passed the five
to Dixon who spread it open with both hands
to let me see it before he put it away.
"And a deuce from me if you'll do it," he tacked on,
taking my greedy silence for resistance.

"Who do I kill?" I said, taking the line
from George Raft, probably.
                              "Look, kid, it's legal.
You *save* a guy!" the tout said in a spout.

"Lay off," said Dixon, and putting his hand on my shoulder,
he walked me off two paces. "It's like this.
The guy's choked full of rotgut and can't heave it.
I tried to stick my fingers down his throat
to get him started, but I just can't make it.
Kid," he said, "it takes guts I ain't got.
You got the guts to try?"
                              And there I was
with a chance to have more guts than a first mate,
and seven dollars to boot!
                              "Which guy?" I said—
only for something to say: I knew already.

"The groaner by the winch. I got a fid
to jam between his teeth if you'll reach in
and stick your fingers down his throat."
                                          We raised him,
half-sitting, with his head back on the chains,
and Dixon got the thick end of the fid
jammed into his teeth on one side. "LET'S GO, KID!"
he screamed, almost as green as the half-corpse
that had begun to tremble like a fish
thrown on the deck, not dead yet, though too dead
to buck again.
                  But when I touched the slime
that might have been his tongue, I couldn't make it.
"Dixon, I can't do it!"
                        "Well, damn your eyes,
you *said* you would. Now put up, or by God
I'll heave you over!"
                      "Wait a minute," I said,
catching my education by the tail.
"Can you hold him there a minute?"
                                    "*If he lives.*
Now where the Hell you going?"
                                "I'll be right back,"
I called, already going, "I'll be right back."

178

I ran for the locker, grabbed the feather duster,
and ran back, snatching out the grimiest feather,
took out my knife, peeled off all but the tip,
then fished his throat with it, twirling the stem
till I felt him knotting up. "Evoe!" I shouted
for Bacchus to remember I remembered,
not knowing till later that I mispronounced it.
"EE-VO," not giving Bacchus all his syllables.

"Heave-ho it is!" roared Dixon and ducked aside
as the corpse spouted. "There, by God, she blows!"
And blow she did. I've never seen a man
that dirty and still alive. Except maybe the tout
clapping me on the shoulder. "You did it, kid!
By God, you did it! Johnny, didn't he do it!"

Dixon wiped his hands on the drunk's back
where he had twisted and sprawled over the winch-drum
(what reflex is it turns a dead man over
to let him retch facedown?) and fished the five
out of his pocket. "Where'd you learn that trick?"
he said as I took the money and waited for more.

I could have told him, "Dmitri Merezhkovsky,
Julian the Apostate," but it wasn't
on Miss Blake's list, and certainly not on his.
"How about the other deuce?" I said instead.

He was holding the feather duster by the handle
and turning his wrist to inspect it from all sides
and looking down into its head of fuzz.
"What's this thing doing on a ship?" he said.

"Waiting for Romans," I told him, guessing his game
but hoping to play him off. "That's history, Dixon.
When a man went to a banquet and stuffed himself,
he'd head for a men's room called a *vomitorium*,
tickle his throat with a feather, do an upchuck,
and then start over. How about that deuce?"

"If you're so smart, then you can figure out
I said if you used your fingers."

                              "Hey," said the tout,
"If you ain't paying up, get back my fin!
If you can welch on this punk kid, then I can!"

"Go peddle your sewer sweat," Dixon said. "Here, kid.
You earned it right enough. Go buy yourself
more education." And stuffed into my pocket
a crumple I unfolded into—one bill,
while he went forward, shoving the tout away.

Six dollars, then. One short. But the first cash
my education ever paid, and that
from off the reading list, though of the Empire,
if not the Kingdom.
                              Meanwhile, the hat passed,
the crowd's roar signalling, the pomade gorilla
came from the Ladies' and pushed up the stairs
from his own *vomitorium* to the orgy
where low sisters of *meretrices honestae*
waited to mount their table through lit smoke
into my nose-to-the-window education
one deck below the Captain's Yankee eye
on watch for the Harbor Cruiser and the tide,
bearing off Thompson Island to the left,
Deer Island to the right, and dead ahead
Boston's night-glow spindled like two mists:
one on the floodlit needle of Bunker Hill,
one on the Custom House, both shimmering out
to sit the waters of Babylon off Boston,
whose dented cup—an original Paul Revere
fallen from hand to hand—I drained like the kings
of fornication, mad for dirty wine.
And for the kingdoms opening like a book.

Cal Coolidge and the Co
(Poem for $98.41 plus, hopefully, bonuses.)

Monday's child in Boston looked like soot
on blackloaf cobbles under the screeching El
on Causeway St. Friday's child looked like fishguts.
Through all the rat-faced week I ever saw
fouling its gutters, Judson Treadlowe Marshall
looked like Calvin Coolidge. Or like a man
who looked like Coolidge looking in a glass
to wonder how he had missed being President.

That's two resemblances, or one and a half,
plus fishguts, soot, and all the mudflat week
in Boston Mass for the saint-misted names
and the frame around them. Add a high stiff collar,
a pin-knot head bookkeeper's tie, a jawbone
bulging with its grip on integrity,
and what you have will do for J. T. Marshall
doing for Calvin Coolidge at about
eleven cents on the dollar
                              —against which I,
hereby, as of this date I sit to write,
being June 30th, 1966,
lay claim to ninety-eight dollars and forty-one cents.
Meaning I'll take more but won't settle for less.
And I've waited long enough. This is the story:

Getting a job in 1933
was family grapevine business. What jobs there were
were hanging out no shingles. You found your door
when someone you knew knew someone.
I was just out of high school with nothing to do
and less than half a start toward college money.
I needed a paycheck anywhere there was one.
After a while John Follo, my *compadre*,
made the connection.
                              John Follo was a barber.
He and my Uncle Alec and Frank Fiore
made half of nothing a week in a ratty shop
under the El, a block south of North Station
and cater-corner from the Biscuit Co.

J. T. Marshall—*Meestra Maresciallo*—
was head clerk at the Co, and what they had
for gentry in the shop. When he walked in
even Frank Fiore stopped bellowing Mussolini
and *Italia irredenta*. Any customer
was one more quarter and maybe a nickel tip
—which was pedigree enough on Causeway St.—
but *Maresciallo* was a *gentilaman*—
a daily shave, a haircut once a week,
and one of the Lords of Life who Hired and Fired.

I used to shine his shoes when I was a kid
squeezing for nickels, but my *compadre* John,
who liked a gesture, never would let him pay me.
And J. T. Marshall, who seemed to like his nickels,
never insisted hard enough to lose one.
Not that I lost out by it—my *compadre*
was not a man to charge me for his gestures.
He always paid for God once God had left.
—But I could still think what I wasn't saying
because the *compadre* would rather it wasn't said.

Who knows what pious drivel and kowtowing
John Follo—rest the sweet soul of a man—
sang and danced to, talking me up to a job
over hot towels, Bay Rum, and Lucky Tiger.
I know I came out of it at least a saint
for J. T. God said yes and I was called
by His elected messenger, my *compadre*,
who took two hours to lecture me half-enough
on the divinity of J. T. Marshall
and on the deference due him.
                              Fair enough.
He needed deference. I needed a job.
I'd trade him need for need.
                              On the Chosen Day
I walked in like a choirboy and sat stiff
as Yessir, Nosir, and Fifty Merit Badges—
thirty-seven of which I did once have
in the first sewing on of an ambition.
Badged, unbadged, but scrubbed to halos, I sat

182

while J. T. read the Sermon on the Biscuit
from Ambition through Integrity to Zeal.
There, while the El trains screamed by unavailing
outside his window and his mottoed wall,
he let me know the future lay ahead.
And though the present started at the bottom,
who knew but what in forty faithful years
I might not sit—well, not at *his* high desk,
but maybe on the same floor, in a corner,
where every day while I was being true
I, too, might keep a motto to its wall.

—And down to business. I got the job.
Shipping room. Night shift. Punch the clock by eight,
work till the trucks were loaded. The good Co,
whose name and prayer were service, guaranteed
next-day delivery. While the shipping crews
wheeled up their carts, Gallagher at the gate
chanted his night-long litany of Kute Kookies
to the crew's antiphon, and three of us
illuminated triplicate manuscripts
of Honey Hunks, Goo Globules, Marshy Mounds
with marginalia of price and poundage
row after row, cross-checking, pulling carbons,
piddling progress through its long subtotals
to its grand nothing at fourteen bucks a week.

And glad to have it. I'd have done more for less.
Though not in virtue's name. Or not as virtue
came memoed down the tube from J. T. Marshall;
concerning which and whom, John Follo told me
my third day on the job, I was to pay him
for a Stetson he had bought for J. T. Marshall
who was too noble to pocket my first week's pay
as his employment fee, but who had chosen—
with some reluctance, I was made to know—
a pearl-gray prize at Hymen's Haberdashers
for which John Follo had paid, for which I owed him
twelve dollars and ninety cents. Well, I had paid
for every cockroach job I ever got.
This time I even saved a dollar-ten.

Such was my dividend from the higher ethics
of Judson Treadlowe Marshall. And four months later
a raise to sixteen dollars.
                                    I was rich:
a dollar a week for carfare, one to spend,
and twelve to bank—at first—and then fourteen.
J. T. could have had Sears Roebuck's best tin halo
if they'd had one to fit him, and welcome to it.

But never doubt I meant to get mine back
in hard cash—and with interest—for hard cash.
Not that I held a grudge. A Stetson delivered
to Old Integrity as the price of the faith
is nothing to hide a bilious night-light under
for thirty-three years. And J. T. God drained dead
into his own glass inkwell years ago.
I wouldn't hold a grudge against a ghost,
not even one that looked like Calvin Coolidge
snitching fedoras and shoeshines from the poor.
It's just that I'd sooner turn a fool to advantage
than lose my advantage of him.
                                    Besides, I promised.
Promised myself, that is.
                                    One August morning
of 'thirty-four (I had been accepted at Bates,
had cash enough to eke out the first year,
and had given notice) I was called upstairs
by Calvin J. T. Coolmarsh.
                                    He had his desk
(as I might have said before, but now will do)
at one end of the aisle, like half an altar
(the lower half) whose glory managed yet
to shine down on the stalls of bent gray saints
at ghostly homage in their Curia.
The wall said: THINK. And: YOU ARE YOUR OWN FUTURE.
And, in four colors: NEW! KASHEW KA-RUNCHIES!

Against the wall, lighting these sacraments,
a hat rack rose resplendent to the Lord
in oak of the True Cross. Upon it shone,
straight to my soul as I sat facing Him,

the Pearlgray Perfect Stetson of Great Price,
its purity undimmed by the dark year.

"College!" the High Priest said. "Well, now. Well, well, now!"
(He liked a round beginning twice around.)
"We like to see a young man get ahead."
(*And old heads get new Stetsons*, the oak whispered,
dancing a little as a train shot by
just at the window, strewing splinters of light.)
"Still, if I'd known you hadn't meant to stay . . .
you know we think of ourselves as a family . . .
I don't know what we'll do for a replacement . . . ."
(*Spit out the window*, I thought of telling him.
*Lift the first hat you hit. If what's under it
can hold a pencil and can see the sidewalk,
that's twice enough for any job you've got.*)
". . . A question of loyalty and clear understanding,
you understand . . . ."
                    I said I understood.
I said I was grateful for the opportunity.
I said my heart would ever be with the Co
and the family of Cal Marshedge and J. T. Coolshell.
He said he would shake my hand and wish me luck.
The hat tree shook again. The Stetson's ghost
called from my *compadre*, "Remember me!"
He said, "Good-bye." I said, "Good-bye, sir. Thank you."
He said, "Be worthy of your opportunity."
—What could I say to that? It choked me up
to think what sentiment was in that man.

I stumbled out the door and into the Waldorf
(the cafeteria, not the hotel).
There, over coffee-and, I sat and wrote
"12.90" and then figured 6%
compounded annually for fifty years
from 1933, and drew a circle
around the last date, 1983,
and wrote "to be collected before then."
And swore it by the oak of the True Hat Rack
until it flower again at the last Easter,
or till the last fool's dead in Boston, Mass,
or till it's eight P.M. at the Biscuit Co

on the eve of the Last Delivery, or until
I had turned one damnfool to my advantage
or lost my advantage of him and gone damned
for being more fool than what I call a fool.
And damned if I'll be so damned.
                                        That's why this poem,
whatever it lacks of merit, won't lack point
if I can sell it to some fool editor
for a minimum of $12.90 at 6%
compounded, as of 1966,
for thirty-three years—which comes out, as I have it
(I don't remember what I figured then
but I called my insurance agent, and take his figure)
to exactly ninety-eight dollars and forty-one cents,
claimed from and for the ghost of J. T. Marshall,
along with such bonuses as may be due me
for having studied the arts of exorcism
(which only a fool, let me insist, will sneer at).

    Postscript

In '68—as I want a ghost to know—
I sold this poem to *Harper's* for two hundred
and fifty dollars. That's cost plus bonuses
plus satisfaction. Jack Fischer wrote to say
it was the most *Harper's* had ever paid
for a single poem. I take that as one more bonus,
and as proof there is a market for exorcism.
I could have bought it myself to run in *SR*,
which would have paid at least five hundred for it,
but it wouldn't have been the same. I wanted the money,
but I wanted someone else to say I had earned it.
How else could I have proven to a ghost
I hadn't been lying to it half a lifetime?

I've marked it Q.E.D., and banked the check,
and awarded myself the Oxford Dictionary
(at 25% off three hundred, list)
and took my wife to lunch at The Four Seasons.
That left me four dollars down, with taxes to pay,
but the books are deductible as office equipment,
and my wife is business, being subject matter,

186

which makes her deductible on a blurred receipt.
I'm afraid that brackets her with J. T. Marshall,
but I'm closing *him* out (so I shall insist
if the Revenuers insist) as a capital gain—
and that's a difference not even he would argue.

That's the account sheet. Someone is always asking
how poets make a living and no poet
has ever written to say. Some years back *Playboy*
asked me to write a piece on just that subject
and offered me fifteen hundred for it. I told them
I tried to live as a poet but made my living
by shrewdness, and had been shrewd enough—with luck
(which means I guessed well on a rising market)—
not to need fifteen hundred. Say it would take
a week of a wrong attention to write that piece:
it comes out as no bargain.
                I've grown pure
in having all I need this side of greed,
and I have more congenial sins to work on.
A man is what he does with his attention
and mine is not for sale, though I'll take cash—
and gladly—for whatever my attention
turns to for its own sake, when I'm finished with it.

Let this be my leave offering to the ghost
of J. T. Marshall, and of twenty others
who bought me cheap, and couldn't afford me now,
because I can't afford to be afforded
by anyone but myself, or I'd lose the ghost
of how I live, however I make my living.

And so to my last bonus, which is the first.
Any man can learn to learn from the wise
once he can find them; but learn to learn from a fool
and all the world's your faculty. I leave here
one ghost lighter but, finally, with a thanks
to the ghost of J. T. Marshall, emeritus,
who left his hat on an unmysterious tree,
but taught me what he didn't know himself.

A Five-Year Step

I don't remember what I was arguing
in H. H. Blanchard's Medieval Lit.
at Tufts in '37—something to do
with numerology, and I knew about it
the way my cousins knew baseball statistics
by having been raised inside them, but couldn't prove it.
"It does sound plausible," said H.H.B.,
"but how do you know if you can't document it?
Remember, we're not discussing how *we* feel
but what went on in the mind of the Middle Ages."

"That's just the point," I told him. "I was born there.
Or else I was born beforehand to where they came."

And if it was half a flourish for sweet style's sake—
not for a class of dolts to titter at
though they had to have their titter, and let them have it—
it still was half as true as I was born.
Maybe half as true as anyone is born,
and with no proven Renaissance to follow.
At least I haven't met Lorenzo's ghost
in any court I've come to, nor Leonardo
at the Academy, nor myself afire
with dawn enough to strike spires from the day.

Sometimes I think I've made it out of the dark
but not into the light. There may be light.
But what's in the Control Rooms is a glow
dim red as altar tapers, and as faithful
to the Holy Ghosts of needles on their dials
trembling with Presences.
                              As I was born—
to dim red glows I sensed but could not read
except to know there are Presences, and to learn
the first of everything is a lunacy
whose chatter starts before us in the dark.

A cave of colored windows where God's light
came down in shafts bored through His core of stone

188

closed me in good and evil, and I was wrong,
my natures all veined sinful before starting.
I felt His eye bore and His great grab reach
to sulfurous ores soul-deep in half my dreams.

And from the rails and galleries of that dark
and at its pitheads, black-flagged orators
of tongues that were never mine sermoned me through
to guilt and the Irish Trinity. Ma wept
to hear how God denied His round Italian
for a nose full of South Boston Jeremiads.
Nights, I could hear her arguing with Pa
to take the matter up with San Michele
or with San Giovanni of his own son's name.
But we couldn't be sure he had made it up that high.
Weren't we still praying him out of Purgatory?
However it was, we never got an answer.

I did what was done to me and fell asleep
falling off roofs and clouds to wake up screaming,
holding my genitals that had fallen off
because they belonged to the Devil and he'd come for them
and changed me into a girl for punishment.
But in another sleep I was all escapes.
I killed Cavalcante who had killed my father—
he shouldn't have driven so fast—and ran back home
and Pa himself was there and gave me wine
in three red glasses, because I was his son.
Himself the tall first number of the bottle
he filled me from. And Ma, an eight, behind him
in the two great circles he had married one.

I didn't know then my dreams were from a mountain
where every town defended its own Virgin
just as the Greeks had left her in a cave.
But I could tell St. Patrick was none of mine,
though at St. Joe's his feast day waved more flags
than God broke out for Easter and Christmas together.

What was I then? Thirteen. Maybe fourteen.
Like Ma, I half believed I was safe in God
and what God we were safe in. I couldn't have guessed

we were Greeks who spoke ourselves in bad Italian
from a parish of goat thickets, civil war,
and hot blood on the mountain—all our saints
disguised as Catholic but as mountain-rank
as a day's sweat on the ledges of the starved
who put their prayers into thickets. I had left
St. Joe's before I left and didn't know it.
It took a clown to rip my thicket loose:
and in came Father Ryan blowing his nose
one warm March day to lather the Sunday School
in his own idea of a hagiological rally
for the Big Green Team. And sent the mountain sliding
down on the cave forever.
                            His nose well blown,
he stood above us, outside the altar rail
and worked the boys up to three last Green Cheers:
"Where did St. Patrick come from?"
                    "Ireland!" the saved screamed.
"And where did he bring his blessing?"
                            Again: "Ireland!"
"And where did your fathers come from?"
                            Once again
he got his chorus but he lost my soul.
I heard a bellowing of lunatic treason:
"FROM ITALY, BY GOD!"
                    And didn't know
I was the lunatic till he grabbed my ear
and dragged me to the altar: "PRAY FOR YOUR SOUL!"

But I'd be damned first. I stamped out of there running
the wronged rage of the blind who have no world
or would sooner knock it over than be trapped.
Later, he said I stamped my heel on his instep.
I won't deny it. He did limp for two weeks.
And world as it was, though I was innocent
by memory and intention, I'd used that trick
a time or two to make a fool let go.

I'd had my skull cracked once for being slow.
And Toots Fitzgerald still has a bad shoulder
from learning I learn fast. He ran me down
with obvious intent to teach me something

190

I wasn't inclined to learn. He was fifteen
and I was a snotty ten the day of our lesson.
Though as it happened, I ended up teaching him
what I hadn't learned myself before I did it.

I took off down the middle of Summer Street
but with too little start. Toots pounded after
five good years faster, and had me, or would have had me
in one more step. But when I heard his breath
hard at my shoulder, I dropped into a ball
and tripped him on the fly. He hit macadam
like a potato sack dropped off a truck
and may have been still skidding by the time
I jumped the Careys' fence and was home safe—
I didn't stay around to pick him up.

His father came that night and wanted Ma
to pay for a doctor and a ruined coat.
But even he, when he saw me, could figure out
Toots had five years, better than twenty pounds,
and at least a foot and a few inches on me.
He had to admit I weighed in as the defender
and that was that. I took my beating later,
when Toots could run again—off to one side:
he'd learned to avoid my wake. And when he caught me,
he only hit for form's sake. Better that
than take a rock in the head when he wasn't looking.

He knew it and I knew it and we were quits.
But I didn't know I knew it till it was done.
And even then I wasn't sure who'd done it
for me or *to* me. Nor even *what* had been done.

The day I broke up Father Ryan's rally
for the Big Green Saint was one more education
in what I hadn't known about myself,
even to guess about, till I lay hiding
among the river cattails, red as murder,
and filling a wax museum with bloody poses
of Trovatore howling down on Carmen
with all blades out and no one giving an inch,
while Rigoletto opened his bloody sack
(that was beside a river, too, I remembered)

and the goddamn Duke, picking up the wrong cue
kept yelling, *"La commedia è finita."*

I played it out, my belly in a knot
and the weather slanting cold into the night.
I'd gone to communion that morning (I could hear
Sparafucile cackling among the damned
to think what day that was) and had had no breakfast.
I didn't dare go home till after midnight.
And didn't dare go then. And almost didn't,
at least in the role I was half sure I was playing.
For a coat and a sandwich, I'd have hopped a trolley,
stolen a first ride into Sullivan Square,
and jumped whatever was heading into Boston
and out the other side. Or so, at least,
I told myself in whatever part I was playing,
knowing, at curtain time, Ma would be waiting.

Those days she was no one to fool with. Some damn cousin
had worked a sheet of leather into a roll,
bound up one end, and cut the rest to cattails.
Ma kept it for tribal sessions. This would be tribal.
Nor had I ever been closer to the tribe
in my own mood. I knew what was coming next—
I thought I did—and thought I had outgrown it
before it happened. Let her play it hot:
I'd play it cold.
              She was sitting in the kitchen
like a stone sybil hissing, the leather cat—
it was my day for cattails—on the table
like a dried familiar, dead but hissing back.
I let her work me over till the welts
bled through my shirt and wouldn't make a sound
except to say, "You having a good time?"
It broke her fit. She was the one to cry.

But everyone played his part in our asylum.
She dropped the cat and stood crying. I picked it up
and tossed it into the garbage. And she kissed me.
And both of us knew it was my confirmation.

—Yes, from *Pagliacci* or from *Rigoletto*.
And yet it was real enough and I was a man,

192

and frightened her. Had it been Italy,
she thought, she might have watched me climb the mountain
as wronged men go to vengeance where they find it—
wherever the madhouse rocks of history
spin out the numbers of whatever they are
and let a fool and the crumbs of what he has
come through to be taken. She could see me dying
with *carabinieri* smoking out their blood
around the rock I leaped from.
                                        It was that—
guessing what mad histories she read me from—
broke my own madness. How could we ever meet?
I had escaped her, though she washed my back
and oiled it, sobbing her first mood in reverse,
and brought me soup and heated-over spaghetti.
I had escaped her. Would she escape me?
I'd sooner have lost the *Iliad* and the *Odyssey*
than the purity of her madness, which was love
in its own numbered cave. I kissed her forehead
and told her to go to bed and she went to bed,
radiant with my found manhood, as if she dreamed
I had killed the *carabinieri*, gotten away,
gone off to sea and the numbers of destiny
to luck's great seven, and home in a Cadillac
chauffered by a Colonel of *bersaglieri*.
I went to bed myself almost believing
I was a man and had snapped ropes in two,
though I half smelled the grease paint of my fraud.
The skin of my back was pulled too tight for wearing,
but I wasn't about to take off up a mountain
that wasn't there. I had my moods to climb.
And had climbed out of them when I'd played them through
till the next lunacy came from the casting office.

—Meanwhile "At Liberty" as unemployed hams
used to announce in *Variety*. Meaning nowhere,
with nothing to do about it but sit and think.
What had been done? Who did what had been done?
It was so small a step from God that morning.
And took me five more years to finish taking,
sometimes in real sweat, sometimes in real grease paint,

and often enough in both. But I had left
the cave forever, even when I went back
still fingering a guilt like the dry scab
of a cut someone had given me. As I left
that cat-of-twenty-tails in a day's garbage,
curling to question marks on the chicken bones,
as if to ask, "Who chooses what we do?"

I found one part of one answer five years later,
and took thirty more to learn there was not much more.

It was a June day. I was home from school
and curled by my window reading William James
on *The Varieties of Religious Experience*
because a nice-nelly neighbor, half a priest,
and home from the seminary, had sermoned me
when he met me coming from the library
and saw it under my arm. Well, I'd *meant* to read it
or I wouldn't have taken it out, but when he horned in
I decided to take notes to needle him with,
and was working at that. Besides, I was having a fling
at being country gentleman. Come Monday,
I'd have to start another summer's gang
jackhammering for the Gas Co—or for diPietro
who subcontracted for the Gas Co's sweat.
It always took two weeks on the damned hammer
before I could hold my breakfast until lunch,
and at night I'd be hitting my bed, too tired for supper.
Then in ten seconds it would be five o'clock
and time to start again. But this was Thursday
and I was still a scholar.
                                        Ma was outside—
my abdicated matriarch and my daughter—
fussing her flowers to bridals by my window.
She was a witch of flowers and could summon them
out of the ground as if they lay full blossomed
and wrapped in mulch, waiting for her to call.
Flowers were her light and gifted as her dark
with tongues she knew, and things did, but no other.
I heard her cooing incantations to them
in the same rhythms I would hear her hiss
when she attacked a dust sent to offend her.

It wasn't enough to scrub it from her floor.
She had to hate it out of the universe.
As she needed now to love her flowers to bloom.
I was taking a killing note on nitrous oxide
("That, by the way," I'd tell him, "is laughing gas.")
and on what the stuff could do for seminarians
who were running short of mystical experiences,
when I heard a step on the walk, and then the nose
you-know-which Father talked through, asking to know
if I was home.
                    I didn't have to be told
what local priestlet had gone to mass that morning
and stayed to discuss my soul with what local nose.
We all came out being crazy our own way.
But Ma got my soul's medal. "Heesa no home-a,"
I heard her say, defending me on my mountain.

It was as good as any laughing gas
for lifting me to a vision. I saw Time
stripped to Plotinus's and Teresa's bones
and built again to walls and terraces
up the whole mountain I had never seen
out of whose caves my acts came looking for me
like the dark and lighted numbers of a fate
stalked by *carabinieri*, while a sybil,
crouched in a thicket, hissed them to the bone edge
and sent them spinning with a bolt of hate.

—A nose blew through my dream and blew it back,
and Father Ryan was pouring it on Ma
to think of her own soul and of the sin
of letting her son be rotted through by evil
till he was pitchforked screaming into Hell
to wail in the broth forever.
                                        Ma didn't exactly
catch all the words but she made out the tune.
If she was my daughter now, she was still a Fury
to any wrong nose that twitched up the mountain.
I heard her scald three thousand guardian years
of a pure mother Arabic, Hebrew, Greek,
Latin, Cave-dialect—you name the tongue
that suffers birth. And if it came out broken

through a slapstick turn of history, it was still
sung from a peak higher than all laughing gases:
"You leava my Johnny alone-a, you Irisha, you.
Heesa goo' boy!"
                    And I was the oaf at the window
when the flowered covenant of language split
to holy truth. I laughed sublimities
and wept whole *fabliaux* for history's daughter
tall from her root of love, my comic source,
my radiant witch of first-made lunacies,
and priestess of the tongues before a man.
"Ma," I whispered, laughing through to prayer,
"I thought you did not know me, nor I you,
but what we are is first milk and last candle,
and indivisibly ahead of thought,
and I am no man till I am your son."

—And closed my great-borne five year step-away
into the first love I identified
my whole way back through time; my first deed done
back to the cave our madness happens from.

The Highest Place in Town

Tufts rises on a drumlin, a pocket of till
fallen from a frayed glacier. Had the ice
sprawled a few miles southeast for the letting go
the Hill might have been an island in Boston Harbor,
had rip tides let it be till piles could shore it
firm to the map.
                    Firm to a map old men
kept in their heads to prove a fall from grace,
it made a mile-long sled-run toward the river
till streets and traffic blackened across sled tracks.
Ed Boggs' grandfather swore by cackling Genesis
back to the winter of 1852
when the snow mushed, then froze a two-inch crust,
he'd coasted from the top, across the river,
up the far bank, and on into the swamp.

I listened but didn't believe. The river meadows
ran flat too far once you were off the Hill.
And how had he made it up that mile of slick
to come down longer than history, the old faker?

I squabbled with Ed, claiming it couldn't be done
and ended having to prove it—on a bike
from the top of Winthrop Street, timed to the light
at Boston Ave, with Ed posted halfway
under the trees to signal on the yellow.
I was out of control a hundred yards down, standing
wind-blinded on the brakes, Reos and Fords
honking and climbing the sidewalk out of my slew
till my front wheel broke on a curb and a hedge caught me.

What had I proved of nothing? Ed still believed.
Ma sold the bike to the next junkman by.
The cops took down my name and never forgot.
Months later they hauled me in for wearing bruises
from a fight I hadn't started. The desk sergeant
roared at me down his finger. "There," he said,
"is the freshest kid in Medford!" "Yeah," I told him,
"I work for Al Capone." But when they clanged me
into a cell, I cried—till my sister came
and I had to play tough again. There were no charges:
it was meant to scare me good. But years later,
when I was peddling house-to-house for pennies
I never got, the cops in Arlington
refused me a permit to wear out shoes for nothing
because the son-of-a-bitch that answered the phone
in Medford knew my name.
                              If men were less,
places were more and haunted by long traces.
The Rez was one. The highest place in town.
Some race of giants Grampa Boggs could fable
had terraced another hill above the Hill
and built a crater lake with a brick bottom
lipped by granite slabs and fenced in iron,
with a brick pump house by the college gate.

It formed, I suppose, the hydrostatic head
that firmed our faucets and let fire hoses roar
their rainbows into steam when the red blinked.

For me it was the next street to the moon
around those upper acres, an Indian prayer
to blue gods in their valley, King of the Hill
down grass slides steep enough to burn, cops baited
over the fence to run slides on the ice
and away on the other side, nights looking down
for stars in black water, first girls walked
tittering around the sky and down again
with nothing said or seen, boy-packs that sat
waiting for time under the Dipper's arm
and went home without it, aching summer's peak
when the town below gasped sleepless while toy breezes
over the top stirred the hung steams of August.
Time, place, and time-and-place. What names come to
on clear sight lines over the topmost elm
below, ago. Not stopped for and not left.

I almost drowned there once when the ice too late
buckled and gulped a leg; but sprawled flat,
crabbed to the edge on a rubbery inch of water,
ran my wet mile home, and sank into a tub
to shiver back through steam while Ma cried
and slapped me and brought me cocoa and cried again.

In 'thirty-three I used to meet Jim Brown there
to talk books at the stars. In one full moon
we were making up ad-copy based on Veblen
when a football player strolled by, his varsity T
worn on his back and inside out.
                                        "By God,"
Jim said, "we make up bad examples, and there goes
the perfect paradigm of Veblen's 'trophy'—
the badge worn with such obvious negligence
that it becomes more obvious."
                                        I was sitting
looking away at nothing long down hill.
I had it in mind that Veblen's tribal feathers
were always worn full plumed. But "paradigm"

198

was a new word to me, and I wanted it
more than another theory. I asked what it meant,
and remember feeling a little disappointed
it hadn't a fancier meaning but liked its sound
and was thinking I could drop it here and there
as a verbal trophy; when I saw a shadow
drop from a tree by the girls' dorm and come past us
and leave its face in the streetlight where Sam Saddle,
who was ten when I was ten, but stayed there,
took home a lank retarded lust whose glands
out-peeped his half mind. Poor man-hulked, boy-dim,
birth-dented skulk of an old hide-and-seek
I left behind a tree where he still played,
but skewed and dangerous in more body than mind.
I watched him lost downhill, off to the night
some cop would tag him out of his own shadow
to cell blocks, while I learned another word.
And sent him, like a prayer, my last learned word:
"God send sweet paradigms of what this is
till the Dipper raise its one hand to a noon
there are no minutes of."
                              "You're muttering,"
Jim said.
            "Sorry. My mind was wandering off
the end of vocabularies."
                              "Maybe a mutter
is the one sound after the last vocabulary."

"Or what vocabularies keep trying to say."

Names. A nameplace. Jim Brown went to work
as an efficiency expert. I went to Bates,
transferred to Tufts, and was back beside the Rez
signed on with the National Youth Administration
to waste time for a federal quarter an hour.
Blue smokey afternoons, the valley's autumn
flaring and rusting north, the iron fence
leaking its shadow to us across the road,
I stood in line with other federalists
on crisps of leaves it was dishonor to rake,
though we had to stir them, and watched Harry Hayford
walk his briefcase like a dog on a choke

to the library and one more inch of note cards
for the term paper I meant to beat him in.
"Go, you sweet bastard, go!" I told a ghost
his shadow left on the leaves, and fell to raking
till the crew hissed and I had to scatter my pile
back on the grass like notes I wasn't taking.

He got his *summa*, damn him, and I missed mine
though I outshouted him whole drunken nights
to prove I had a better thesis going,
or a better bellows for what thesis I had.

Did a little dog's briefcase laugh to see a hill
go over the moon and down again to time?
I had a friend and roared him comedies
as idioms of intention where a stone
dropped by a glacier and gnarled round by roots
is still an echo frozen to a tree.
A namesake locked in place. A word that stays.

It was on the Rez in 1937
I first met Roethke. He and John Holmes, my teacher,
father, friend, and host to my blowfly eggs,
had taught together at Lafayette, and Roethke
was passing through. I was reading on the grass
when John called to me and said the hulk beside him
was Roethke, and told Roethke, stretching a point,
I was a poet.
                                    I think I said hello
but my throat clicked shut on it. Aside from Holmes
I'd never been near enough to talk to a poet.
And couldn't get near enough then, though there he was.
He asked if I was an athlete. I said No.
He asked my fraternity. I said NYA,
and grinned, and hated myself. There must have been more,
but all I remember from a first of princes
was "No" and one limp quip and—I guess—"Good-bye";
though the next night he looked at some of my poems
and didn't tell me entirely how bad they were.
I was beginning to guess that for myself
but couldn't say it to a prince and a stranger.

200

I saved it for John Holmes, though not even he
could guess what confessional I'd built around him.

Holmes was key and keyboard. I'd gone to Bates
looking for something and got myself moralized at
and knew that wasn't what I'd been looking for.
I did find Keats—a gift from Roger Fredland—
and heard "the silver snarling trumpets chide,"
"the music yearning like a god in pain."
I was on an aching jag for the free float.
The first poem I turned in for Holmes to praise
(what else do we mean when we ask for criticism?)
was about seeing sharks in Long Island Sound
and being haunted by them—by anything.
"A sense of process, a name of the hunting sea
haunts me," I wrote. Holmes wrote back in the margin:
"All right; you're haunted. When does it haunt me?"

I was never pretty again in any mirror.
I began to learn music comes off the piano
ten-fingered from eighty-eight keys, and that all the god
that yearns in pain speaks that arithmetic
or only burbles. If that seems little to learn,
I haven't finished learning it; nor that love
is the highest place in town, its country spread
to memorize till every name's in place
in its own ghost, returned exact as music.
Time, place, and time-and-place.

                                 The Rez came down.
Chain-belt gulpers ate the terraces
down to the roadway. Graders scoured a mall.
Cranes reared and nodded, girders in their jaws.
Bricks climbed the steel. The college crossed the street.

Forty feet down from sky, two arms of dorms
reached down a new field, and Carmichael Hall
crossed them at a perspective's end, not well—
Tufts, alas, is an architectural sin.

Holmes died. I went to Tufts to fill a chair
that took his name. I was housed in a new dorm
just about where I guessed the ice had broken

one day I didn't die, a long cut down
from the shortcut Holmes walked across the sky
home from the college. My first night in that room
I thought I saw the leg I dropped through ice
still dangling from the ceiling. John Holmes strolled
over my head looking at everything
in another world.
              I went to Carmichael Lounge
to talk to students, a fumble of good intentions.
My first day there a fat boy asked a question
that still droops like a dead flag into weathers
nothing can breathe. "How does it feel," he said,
"to be a success?"
              I sat a dead man's chair
trying to name mortality to an oaf
too pink-eared to begin. What bones lay buried
that hill down from a sky-top lost! Moon over
a January wood ticking with cold
and round an iron fence with stars boxed in it
Whiteside came at me. How could I have guessed
he meant to marry her?—that bed was mine.
And still he came on round a fence of stars
like a sign from a warped zodiac: *Sponsus* flaming,
the Bridegroom in ascendance, *Virgo* fallen,
Amicus in eclipse under the wheel
that turns men queer and sad and caught between
loves and ironies, mad as the stars once beat
another kind of reason for what we are,
yet feeling what we feel as if it were real.

I had a friend and froze to a dumb question.
My toes were ice cubes. Membranes in my nose
glazed sharp when I breathed in. What comedy
was turning numb and sad? A lie could turn it.
Could I turn from the lie and not be damned?

I heard him quoting from a horoscope:
"You owe me the truth."
                      "I owe you something better."
"I'll settle for that."
              I heard an idiot tell him,
and nothing moved.

                    "You wanted the truth," I said.
"That's half of it. If you want the other half,
I'm sorry but not guilty. I mean sorry
for as good a reason as yours."
                              "I know," he said,
but nothing moved.
                    I thunked my mile downhill
like January wood. The wind behind me
rattled the dead hedge that had caught me once
on the way to proving nothing. "Thanks," I told it,
and made it home again, almost in reason,
if there was reason and we were parts of it.

We never again were friends. A hill came down.
Somebody died. An idiot asked a question
of the idiot who gave answers. A name went out
like candelabra blown to smoky letters.
John Holmes came ambling home over the sky hump
counting miles out from the wind in no hurry,
looking at everything in his own time.

"Evening, Inspector Holmes. What's that out there?"
"A world, sir. Mine."
                    "Inspector, what is a world?"

"A world—as even you might see by looking—
is three steps out to God: first green, then blue,
then purple."
              "Then God, Inspector?"
                                      "And then God."
"In any direction?"
                    "Just one: out from the center."
"Out—there?"
              "Out there as well as any."

"Well now, Inspector, you'll note I pointed to Stoneham.
Are you ready to claim for the Unitarian *logos*
Stoneham is the last purple step to God?
—Remember purple turns to green when you get there."
"And green to blue again, and blue to purple,
and still three steps to God."

                    "Inspector Holmes,
why does the question change from where it is
to wherever you happen to be, once you have gone there?"

"That, sir, is called the mystery."
                              "It sounds shifty.
But as long as God stays Unitarian
the question's academic. Which allows me
to get back to the center, which is: how are you?
what sort of day have you had?"
                              "A good three-stepper
at an altitude above you mundane types.
Come over later: a batch of new books came."

And went home then. Calling a name and no answer.
A habit that had been love. Well then, a drink.
Whatever is after nothing. Hell, take the bottle
and up to the study a while . . .
                              and the woman there.
Red-handed. Wrists slashed. And what she had swallowed.
All propped in a chair in the middle of the room,
three walls of books torn down to rubble round her.
An anatomy of motives stated: *Over
my dead body.* Said in that one room,
the one he closed the door to, never again
alone there. A suicide not good-bye
but a staying change. *Whenever you come again
I will say this to you again who am here forever,
married closer than love, the door flung wide.
And what will you see when you dare look?*

                                        Ah, John,
what faces faces change to down from love,
the highest place come down: a fat oaf there
fumbling sincerities that only smudge
the three-colored country out to mist!
You should have been a Wordsworth of unevent
in a little country of kindness, real or not,
but changing only from green to blue to purple
to the last mist that changes when we near,
success forgiven, every failure love
that cannot fail what it forgives, that dies

finding the name that says us, real or not,
still sounding at the center of the mist
that thinks itself: time, place, and time-and-place.

Ghosts a ghost lives by. Gone from but not left.

The Graph

By time and after, where the guessed-at dead
curled in, unborn, and charred before they hit,
or blew to gases when their tanks cooked off,
or only passed forever through one cloud;
we manned wired systems, and the diagrams
wavered on blue mirages like decals
washed off a sunken panel, whole but warped.

What do the dying die to? Lost names plunged
a graph of smoke like a Black Friday crash,
and told names flipped a toggle's bombs away.
Pig-iron carcasses followed falling. Hammers
an atmosphere away beyond dogged hatches
banged on the pressured roof. A slant of comets
fell off the long sky home. Peeled sores of towns
stained photos magnified to the misty grain
then focused back to what detail showed through
—never the dead—to paper orderlies
who plotted, dot by dot, a guessed-at graph:
MAN HOURS OF PRODUCTION INTERDICTED.
(Generals are phrased by clerks.) And month on month
we hit more shacks and paddies than factories.
The graph wormed nowhere at the foot of the cliff
the dead scrawled down the statistician's eye.

Is dying anything? We buried names.
A clerk with a wet rag was priest enough
for last rites at the crewboards. Each wiped name
proved us our own, one number nearer home,
and never near enough. Our own lies dreamed us.
I practiced thinking I had died last week
and could relax with nothing more to lose.

Still in the night sweat before every mission
a wet rag whispered: "By this time tomorrow
you may have burned to death." My kept name cried
over a surf-soughed sea-cliff to Orion
sinking to tops of salted scrub-pine shadow:
"Then what do I want tonight, if I could have it?"
And having scoured from galaxies to the cellar
of the last bone, it found man's three last wishes
just as the wiped names left them in their dream:
"A woman, whiskey, and a T-bone, rare."

I didn't die, nor did I get my wishes
this side of life again and a sea across,
though every landing back from fantasy
I got two shots of the Flight Surgeon's rye
(Imagine dying on anything less than bourbon!)
and told my tale, the nothing I could tell
of the last sighted names, of slanting comets,
of kills and probables and bombs away,
and diagrams that rippled off still whole.

We went neat courses to graph-numbered reasons:
what Mitsubishi's lathes could not turn out,
no gun could fire; what his assembly lines
could not assemble, never would take off.

But though we put our cross hairs on his roofs,
wind frayed the bombing tables. The jet stream raged
past our last given numbers. The dead went down
steeper than bombs to nothing. Three months' dying
the stalled graph stuck.
                    Then a two-star LeMay,
(later he went to four and then to clinkers)
a wet cigar butt in his carcass jaw,
took over the graph: machines we couldn't hit
were run by men, and men who sleep in houses
can be burned out. We went in low at night
loaded with firesticks we spewed out like nails
from busted kegs, and, with an edge of wind,
scabbed fifty-two square miles of Tokyo.

The graph took off for heavens of fantasy
slide rules compound like prayer wheels. God shall learn

His last from statisticians. One of ours
had beeped back home for fire-insurance tables
of prewar Tokyo, drawn an overlay,
and marked our drop-points where the rates were highest.

His numbers and two stars in God's own wind
set off a firestorm in the tinder flats.
A clerk cartoonist drew flames on the graph
where it charred up the numbers. (Generals
are taught to laugh by clerks.) But all I saw
looked like a city dump burning at night
below a bluff.
                Somewhere inside the mist
of the last grain at its last magnification
rats of our hot statistics sniffed a panic,
dancing their circles on the shrinking darks
to writhe there twitching when the air gave out
inside the firewall cones like little Fujis
spewing an emperor's holiday of sparks,
until the sucked-out air sucked in the firewalls
to gasp up blowtorch flues burned in the sky.

—I guessed this much by linking fossil facts.
What I saw sank to nothing much behind us:
sparks of a burned-out graph, its dots and dashes
disjointed, never visible, and not ours.
So, death surmised from bone—as anthropologists
guess out a face for the Neanderthal.

The one death I will swear I knew the face of
that dying year—knew it as if I were
its own ghost to the end—was F. X. Mannion's,
Foxy Mannion, our altar-boy navigator
who prayed his odds like Stations of the Cross,
a rosary to the number, his map-table
so Christopher'd and Virgin'd and be-Jesus'd
he had to hold his pencil in his teeth
or never draw a course this side of Heaven.

God keep clear Angels plotted to His stars
and draw man's line straight on the Rose of Winds
across blank parallels and meridians,
and call him out and back, and let no blast

deflect his courses, and let F. X. Mannion
be suffered whole where certainties are solved.

I send this prayer to faiths I do not need
for the boy Mannion, saint of his own terrors,
who never linked two words wholly his own
but blurred a quivering *Credo* at every flak burst,
a *Paternoster* at every Zero sighted,
and, when the hammers pounded on the roof,
fisted a scapular and unreeled to God
at a thousand mumbo-jumbo r.p.m.'s
whole litanies recorded at slow rote
where adolescents at the sulphur-stinking
guilt edge of flesh fall to their lonely sin
in God's eye and the terrors they are taught.

Still, more or less, by our asylum rules
he passed for normal—meaning he'd made it back
as often as he'd left—till the payday night
he broke the crap game at the Officers Club.
He had twelve thousand in the Day Room safe,
all labeled and rubber-banded and receipted,
when he woke up next morning sweating terror.
He'd had a dream that luck is a fixed ration.
An Angel or his Virgin Mother had warned him:
luck used up on dice comes off the odds
that keep men on the roster. When night came
he drew his cash for the high-roller wipe-out
against the first-night kings from all four Groups.
He went for broke on every long-side odds.
He rolled and let it ride pass after pass.
When the game broke, he had to take his shirt off
and wrap the greenbacks in it like dirty laundry.
And when he woke, his next green morning sweat,
his new receipt read forty-seven thousand.

"My God," he told me, sweating, "I tried to *lose!*"
—He lied, of course. No one *can't* lose at craps.
But he was young and greedy and drunk on luck
he'd never known and had to take as guilt.

He was up for that night's mission. God only knows
what r.p.m.'s of litany he spun

over the line he reeled in from the stars
and inched on his mercator to Nagoya.
It broke off there. And if death's guessable,
I'll stake my own—take all or any part—
I heard his final record spun so fast
its grooves outflamed the firewash he dove spieling:
O Holy Mary, Mother of God, I knew it!
O-Holy-Mary-Mother-of-God-I-knew-it!
oholymarymotherofgodiknewit!
—beeping through circuit hum and the squeal of space.

Message received: guilt makes the dark that comes
out of all averages. If men can bear
the mathematics of which they are the chances,
nameless as particles, this was a boy
in the boy rites of war, and he died rich
of all he could not spend of his own guilt.

And if I raid him for a foolish fact,
he did not need his own death, and I do.
For though I studied dying all that year,
saying its names to memory and the moon,
the only dead I saw were souvenirs
from a marine's grimoire, or a saint's dreambook,
or Hieronymus Bosch drunk in the devil's tank,
where corpses shed their living tongues to dark.

I have their telling from the globing moon.
The Quonset snored and sweated. Half down a bottle,
I took a blanket, flashlight, cigarettes,
and filled my canteen at the Shinto Shrine,
half-seas over in the full moon spill.
Two walls and a chow-lion glowed from shadow
as hands and numbers float a wristwatch dial.
The ground crew's tents were pyramids on sticks,
or geometric icebergs in a searchlight:
two facets glaring and two darks asleep.

Drink to what glares from dark. Rays like pale slats
crisscross and cannot hold it. It walks on drums.
The whistle of its whim through decoy angels
blasts hot dawns from their silos. Stickmen dance

through aureoles under it. And at the treetops
black Boanergeses gun it. Their red spit whinnies
across the coral, powdering drifts of ghosts.

Drink to it—to anything. Rye sinks in its bottle.
A drunk sprawls on a beach under a sea-cliff
white as the skull of Argos, socketed
with all the hundred burned caves of his eyes.
I see the moon: a lit tank of sauterne
that stays filled as it spills, the wine aglow
through all the hunch of sea past a black headland.
What cannot find us in the dark of heaven
will have its ray tonight. I see the island
black-etched and sea-lace-trimmed on the lit spill,
home-clear in the hunter's eye. Drink to the hunter.
Four fingers from the bottom the wailers wind
a cyclone up the sky and itchy fingers
poke flak holes high in nothing. I pick a cave,
bottle in one hand, flashlight in the other
—and there were all the dead I ever saw
that dying year, where the flamethrowers had left them
blown back to the inner wall and toppled over
on one another, sizzled too dry to rot,
or so I guessed (and maybe sea-air salted).
Which pocket of Hell was that? Drink to them all.

A tourist there before me had left a keg.
A minute in Hell and all arrival's over.
Sledges, miles off, thumped rock. Spent flak
pattered white dust-ghosts from the ledge. I sat
(two minutes in Hell and any man is home
with nothing else to do) and played my beam
over the damned, and all were duplicates:
heads back as if from broken necks, mouths gaping
wider than they had faces for. A cord
of stacked saints waiting for their horn, or hellkins
discharged from God's will to wait back to dust.

Drink to Malebolge! "Hey, Brother Francis,"
Four Roses called through Hell, "You there, corpse lover,
scraping your flesh to God and the biota
between love's hair shirt and Old Body Grease—

we're down to what comes after all kissed sores.
Which of these would you be, old amateur,
could you have your God-druthers?—this one?"
I beamed him a ray to choose by. "Like this one better?"
I lit another gasper and heard the thudding
change to trip-hammers. "No, no. Two knocks for yes.
One knock for no. Don't mumble." The thudding slackened.
"That's better: space your answers.—How about this one?"
I lit another and heard *thud-thud-thud.*
"No triple thumping," I warned. But still no answer.
"You there—Hieronymus Bosch. Yes, you on the left—
you think I wouldn't know your face in Hell?—
which one of these is Francis at his dream's end?
This one, you say?" I sucked the bottle dry,
beamed in on a gape that had no bottom to it,
and heard the bottle drop, bounce, and not break,
sucking the whiskey out of me into dark:

inside the mouth hole of the gaping mummy
a light-tipped tongue wagged chittering!
                                        Then the rat
leaped out and blurred away across the dark
faster than I could follow with my light.

A half-hour into Hell and most is known.
Two other tongues wagged and went skittering
before the raid thumped out, the All Clear sounded,
and I went sober Sunday'd to the moon
preaching what saints are made of, who can't rot
but only wait God's leaping word out; preaching
all Hell's a sot's rave till, the All Clear sounding,
it's a rat heaven, each in his lived-in feast,
his meat mine of safe blisses to eat out
till light shines through the skin of what we are,
and dotted boys and signing generals,
and moonbone saints aglow above a dark,
all wag a heaven tongue that none can speak
till all do, and in idiom.

                    I climbed back
and lived, my numbers changing their years out

to guessed-at dots of what there is to graph;
and write what I remember of the dead,
our duplicates and their own in the globing moon.

Two Saints

White toga'd God of the gold sandals
that do not touch; Grandfather Mercy
to good boys in their lantern of prayer;
to the evil in me, Thunder—oh Whirlpool Eye
whose mote I was down lenses and spiral tubes
where spun light came apart and I fell through
to the terrible otherness I must become
who could not become myself—this last time down
the lens turned backwards to queer dwindling points
I exorcise the terrors I died small of
there in my midge-days' madness.
                              Small?
The size there was. Your spider was dream enough;
its web, a continent. You, First Father Guilt
forever cocked at the center, my sleep tossed
on the threads of your least stirring.
                              My made guilt
made me food. And then idea. Idea, Father,
is to grapple, not forgive. And what had I
to wrestle thought to, blackfriar'd as I came
past pitch and rumor? Your black priests lessoned me:
good served no good without their laying on:
St. Joe's was the one door and Hell the parish
of every other: though they were friends and kind,
no prayer could save them. But could I have a friend
and say yes to his damnation? deny a friend
and not be damned?
                              When Willie Crosby drowned,
I followed in my tears to a wrong church
I dared not enter, knowing the ground would open
to gulp me burning, or lightning cinder me.
I could not kneel by my friend. He was wet forever,

the light slammed in his eyes, his hair flowing
in tanks of Hell—who had done no wrong, and had lent me
a dime I could never repay but gave for him
to Ralph, the beggar, who sat his legless wait
on a four-wheeled shelf by Woolworth's, offering pencils
it would be death to take.
                              Were his legs buried?
Would he be ghosted to them in fathering time
and walk where Willie swam after all chances?
Is accident a thing?
                              "God wanted Willie,"
the priest told me.
                              And chose *that* way to call him?
Knowing he wasn't even a Catholic?
A boy to murder and then send to Hell?

"All things are in His will."
                              He *meant* it?
—I saw the cramp like an aimed shark in clear water.
I saw God squeeze my friend into a fist,
then drop him blue-pale in a sleep of weeds
till the black grapple stirred him, not awake.

. . . And if there is no accident? Oh spheres
crystals and bells and spires of a planned light
I tried to see by, the meridian blaze
that hurls the godless dark, not of Its will
but theirs, the dark within them
returning of itself to its own nature,
all purposed, all purposeful . . . . No, I could not believe.
If all was God then half of God was evil.

"Ah, blasphemy! Will you dare ask God His reasons?"
said the shadow in the confessional.
                              Could I dare
ask less of anything? I was half damned,
but could not give Willie up.
                              And then forgot him.
Forgot the tears of my first heresy.
I stood alone at the stone-shadowed door
of a wrong church and watched a box go in,
the door swing shut its oak-carved cross on traffic.

A crack ran through the right arm of the cross
and still the cross stayed whole. Seemed to stay whole.
I saw the crack reach gaping through the world
and Willie falling in to a root tangle.
And left before the door opened again.

And then forgot. I had my dog to love,
a year to turn. A madness like a nature
closed seamless as water over a day's drowning.
My legs were animals with themselves to run.
I could not die forever in a thought.

But I had thought a dying up to God
in His confessional, and what was whispered
had been no father to me, though I prayed
as I was whispered. Why did He send me thoughts
that turned to sins? I had not asked to think.
If doubts came, were they mine? I prayed for lilies
out of His garden and was sent a thicket.
If what He sent was sin, whose was the sin?

And still my legs were their own animals
and ran me into light where I forgot,
being glad of energy and half self-solved:
if evil was His sending, how could I
be other than He made me, safe and free
from the boy killed to show me what He meant?

"Of the objectivity of self," said Kiro
a whiskey time later, "take the Siberian sparrow
that lit on a fresh cow flop in February
and there sang spring songs till it froze to the turd.
If man's no bird, he'll take what heat he finds.
I'll be your dollop of truth: nest in the thought,
you shivering fluff: it steams the better for stinking:
man's what sings his accidents to conclusion."

"No," I said, "to conclusions."
                              "That's just to say
there are many plops in the pasture. There's just one
      weather.
And only the same bird always from like eggs.
Take your own case, you lost Dominican

drizzle of second reasons: had your father died
when you were seven and wanting your mother back,
you'd have been guilty of having wished him dead.
When he happened to die, you would have been his killer.
I'll bet a beatification or thirty-two cents—
whichever you think you can deliver first—
you'd be in skirts today, beating your chest
to be sure God had an earful of your guilt,
and preaching others guilty—that's accidence.

"But come to the altar purified for praise,
you'd sing off-key. And back in your saint's cell
there'd be cobwebs on your prayer book, but manuscripts
of notes on canon law. *That* is conclusion:
wherever accidence takes you, it's your conclusion
to sing off-key and nit-pick among loopholes.

"As it happened—accidence—the old man kicked off
while you were still all sour milk and sweet love,
and all the guilt you ever felt was taught you
like another language you never could pronounce,
you lucky bastard. And still, you self-concluded
word-dizzy shyster, you swindle among footnotes,
and can't sing Cause on key. Since God hasn't,
I damn you personally. Now have a drink."

I had the drink. Ah, Kiro, could I pour
a sweeter rhetoric than any I heard
from God's anointed mouths, I'd make a psalm
of the dancer in his arc, of a style of time
to an Okinawan cross; of man, the monstrance
of a pig-iron fragment that might as well
have cut a leaf from a tree; of my friend, the dancer,
dead in the epilogue of an island war
in which no shore was home, nor the sea, place.

A man's what recognizes accident
as the environment. Born of his chances,
dead of the last, his interim is style,
which is to say, his way of choosing reactions
to chances that do not kill, his contract made
with killing chances—a principle of selection
selecting itself.

Kiro, I need to say this,
no longer to you. A saint with a sense of humor
might carve dice from his bones and pray with those.
If his mind was easy—as no saint's is entirely
in the idiom of God—he'd spare himself
by borrowing used bones and rolling those.
Why amputate for nothing? The point is not
to see how much can be lopped and the man live,
but to note the numbers turning into fact.

Kiro, you damned me once and in good whiskey.
Would you again, if out of another bottle
I take you for that easier saint, not saved
but selfless?—in ego, a companion of egoes:
not ego itself, but ego recognized
as an animal attachment, an organ of guess,
the failure that forgives by its own flaws
recognized in another? And then danced to
because the man's a dancer in his own conclusion
after all accidence—If that's half a creed,
its graces are fact, scope, and irony.

"Feet, soap, and idiocy," I heard his ghost
chuckle inside my head. "One blind boy saint
to crack a hole in the dark. And now a blind man
to lead you to the light. That's hagiography?
You're still a swindler, bless you—or be damned:
whichever it is you always really wanted.
I never knew which for sure, nor ever can now."

"I wanted to be sane. Saner at least
than what I'd come from. And I wanted to love.
Want to. And can. And do. You, among others."

"Then drink up. Thirst's a blessing. And when the bottle
smashes on the last number, that's not damnation,
but no mouth, and no saying, and no thirst
—till some damned fool a shadow might have loved
tries stirring up the shadow that isn't there."

I forget what Willie looked like. I see his bottom
shinnying trees above me, hands packing snowballs,
my liver-colored dog that ran between us,

a bubble up from weeds. And that door shut
on a church that could poison me like the black idea
of a drowned boy wasted inside its wrongness,
yet something like a saint, having gone so far.

And because his dying changed my first of reasons.

As Kiro changed to words in a bad letter.
"Hey, by the way, you remember Kiroiates—
weren't you two sort of chummy?—the poor bastard
got it on Okinawa. Grenade fragment.
I hear he's up for maybe a pretty good medal—
if you happen to have a taste for the posthumous.
He always was a classy son-of-a-bitch.
I wish I'd known him better. Well, so it goes.
Don't you go bucking for ribbons. This war's over
with only some strictly surplus dying left."

Do I remember him chuckling in my head?
—"I've seen worse epitaphs and heard worse advice.
Anything's better than what governments write
and G.I. crosses. Imagine *me* under a cross.
The goddamn least a grateful country could do
for its more articulate drunks, dead in Supply,
is to leave a space on dog tags that codes out:
'Religion: bourbon. Marker: broken bottle.'"

. . . Yet something like a saint, having come so far
to change me to a good I had once prayed for
and never reached but by the revelation
a man is in the dauntlessness of style.
The kindness of defeat that quips to graces.
To a dead boy and a dead man in my head
I loved and half forgot, loved and remembered.

I doubt there is much more to what we are.

Epilogue: The Burial of the Last Elder

He died in unknown tongues. Latin he'd heard
the lifelong Sunday cant and cadence of

but not the words, came, mispronounced, to pray him
between a brogue and its South Boston slur,
but right enough, being as far as God.
English he hadn't learned in seventy years
walked round his name. He was the last where none
could sing the yokel cadence of his mountain—
not dialect but defeat, a tribe's long waste
from father stones it could no longer read;
and still a man's first-said good morning home
where light's the mother-door, where all deaths go
their last breath back, what no man leaves for long.

He'd never left but only stretched a visit
into a way of life on a tourist visa
that never quite expired—until he heard
a cock crow and his dog bark and remembered
they were dead in another country a world ago;
but idioms yet a while, as all tongues are
spoken by memory to a habit of hearing.

An idiom closed. That night above New York,
stacked up above a fog, I found Arcturus
off the Big Dipper's handle, then faded down
from galaxies to mist and landed nowhere
down sight lines of blind instruments, and so home—
wherever that is that the dead ignore.

I buried mine and took my own away.
Sweet mornings to the mountain that begins.
Good dancing and good wine, its feast day come.
Goodnight to sons gone down a sea away
and washed back to the stones of a first name.
He lived where nothing meant but only stood
between him and returning, and had forgotten
how to return except as bones must stir
a dust made for them they themselves will make
till names come off the land, and then, and after.

And had forgotten he had never left.

I took my own away. What shall I hear
my last hark back to time? Not where I live.
Nowhere I happen to be. Not where I was.

I never lived anywhere but by accident,
and never went anywhere I meant to stay
till I found I owned a house and lived in it
between jets anywhere. And never knew
my neighbor on either side until the day
my garage roof burned. And never saw either again,
though sometimes a horn honks and an arm waves
and I wave back, not quite sure what I mean,
not sure to whom I mean it.

                    I keep an idiom,
and stay another day and then another,
stretching a tourist visa past the stones
that settle into habits, landmarks noted,
the little place just off the avenue
where someone was young once, and the young still go
in their other idiom, though the easy streets
a walk-up to a love-ago are dangerous
in sentiment and fact, now animal shadows
crouch, hooked to habits they must kill to keep,
tourists of their own means to heaven a while.

I have nowhere to come from or return to,
or when I do go back, it isn't there.
The house is paid for and that's home enough.
Resident persuaders in panel trucks
roar from bullhorns, swearing me to live here.

What could I tell my dead of what I do?

Last month I caught a cab in Philadelphia
bound for Penn Station. A bullhorn roared for Nixon.
The street jammed shut. I paid the cabby off
and wedged my way afoot to catch a train
to where I could vote No. I jumped it
its first wheel round, slid into a seat, slid back
eleven years: I was walking my wife through Rome
the night a salmon-run came lunging
up electronic falls to Piazza Venezia,
and fishermen came howling from every bank,
dove into the boil, and lunged there with the salmon
up a cascade of blather. I remembered

Quasímodo droning lipless through the mask
a Sicilian mother-sybil left him: "The Greeks
invented civil war. The Italians, alas,
perfected it." There up the amplified falls
perfected art roared in the rage of Cause.

"Good Lord, what's that?" my wife said.

                             The falls bellowed:
GIUSTIZIA (*screeeeeee*) IL POPOLO (*scru—oook*).
AGGIORNAMENTO (*iiiiiigh*) ITALIA (*glooorp*)
"Artifacts of perfected art," I told her.
"What?" she cried in the roar. "What did you say?"
"Visible mercy: a war I don't have to go to."
"WHAT?"
             "POLITICS. ABSOLUTION POLITICS."
Around the corner: "Did you say absolution?"
"Yes. Mine. From slogans I don't have to shout."

But could I have told my dead in Heaven or Hell
what I was doing in 1948
six cascade nights a week for Henry Wallace
in the perfected barreling of a cause
I couldn't myself believe but by outshouting
the calms of mind names come to when they come,
closer than salmon run their falling water?"

Two months and a week or two before November,
having been granted an evening with The Man
as my reward for frenzy, I lay awake
knowing the man was wrong, the Cause sold,
and that my calendar was signed and sworn to
for another sixty nights in the cascades
I was the bullhorn of . . . and lunged my way
toward nothing, up Columbias I was trapped in
till—the confessional and November come,
the curtain closed behind me—I made my cross
for Truman, and went home from Cause forever,
in idiom with the dead, whose shrug forgives
wrong sons the imperfect art of being men.

I was still walking backwards from absolution
a first block up the Corso, when my window

flashed neon: TRENTON MAKES—THE WORLD TAKES.

What made me think of Perry in '44,
my bearded con-man beach-rat buddy stripped
to shorts and GI boots and a tan so native
he could have passed for the dawn age in decay?
Outside our mess hall three black boiling troughs
steamed absolution—soap, disinfectant, rinse—
and the loin-clothed rabble stank by in the roar
of sanitation to dip its mess kits pure,
cautious as sinners in their bowing hour
before the power locked in the sacrament.
Till a replacement in full uniform
and even creases, slammed his kit in the boil,
spraying a scald, and Perry jumped back yelling:
CHRISSAKE WATCH WHATCHA DOING! THAT'S
    HOTCHA MEATHEAD!

The oaf glared at the bum: WHYNCHA WEAR PANTS?
And Perry, from the throne of his contempt
for fools still dressed for Sunday School in Hell:
PANTS ARE NO PROTECTION AGAINST IGNORANCE.

DUTCH BOY, the window said. COVERS THE WORLD.

SHE MAY LOOK INNOCENT, said a latrine poster,
BUT PROTECT YOUR PANTS.
                    And then the window again:
HAD YOU BUILT IN BRUNSWICK YOU WOULD BE HOME NOW.

. . . Over the waterfall roaring of the wheels,
slogan by slogan to a town called home . . . .

At Stelton I thought of a traveler from Thackeray's Brussels
(not Smedley—he had bought his horses and fled)
climbing a church tower out of cannon range
of Waterloo, and watching through a glass
deaths so small their uniforms stayed neat
though whole men were ripped out of them.
                              May I learn
a mercy beyond recruitment. I have folded
my last dead to their names and have no father.
Let what I love outlive me and all's well.
Bless everyman his wandering never home.

Bless him his dead and fold them to a name
he can pronounce his last breath back, and keep him
the tourist of his means, toward heaven a while.

I have no worlds to change and none to keep.